7.50 nset

Ponkapog Edition

THE WRITINGS OF
THOMAS BAILEY ALDRICH
IN NINE VOLUMES
WITH PORTRAITS AND MANY ILLUSTRATIONS

VOLUME IV

Thomas Bailey Aldrich
From a photograph by Marshall in 1875

THE WRITINGS
OF
THOMAS BAILEY ALDRICH

PRUDENCE PALFREY AND
A RIVERMOUTH ROMANCE

BOSTON AND NEW YORK
HOUGHTON, MIFFLIN AND COMPANY
THE RIVERSIDE PRESS, CAMBRIDGE
1907

COPYRIGHT 1873, 1901, 1902 BY THOMAS BAILEY ALDRICH

COPYRIGHT 1874 BY JAMES R. OSGOOD & CO.

COPYRIGHT 1907 BY HOUGHTON, MIFFLIN AND COMPANY

ALL RIGHTS RESERVED

CONTENTS

PAGE

PRUDENCE PALFREY

I.	IN WHICH PARSON WIBIRD HAWKINS RETIRES FROM BUSINESS	3
II.	A PARSON OF THE OLD SCHOOL	10
III.	MR. DENT AND HIS WARD	22
IV.	DRAGONS	29
V.	THE ROMANCE OF HORSESHOE LANE	47
VI.	CONCERNING A SKELETON IN A CLOSET	70
VII.	HOW JOHN DENT MADE HIS PILE AND LOST IT	90
VIII.	THE PARSON'S LAST TEXT	113
IX.	A WILL, AND THE WAY OF IT	127
X.	THE NEW MINISTER	141
XI.	A NEW ENGLAND IDOL	153
XII.	PRUE!	166
XIII.	JONAH	183
XIV.	KING COPHETUA AND THE BEGGAR MAID	191
XV.	COLONEL PEYTON TODHUNTER	201
XVI.	HOW PRUE SANG AULD ROBIN GRAY	220
XVII.	HOW MR. DILLINGHAM LOOKED OUT OF A WINDOW	232
XVIII.	AN EMPTY NEST	242
XIX.	A RIVERMOUTH MYSTERY	260

A RIVERMOUTH ROMANCE 269

ILLUSTRATIONS

THOMAS BAILEY ALDRICH. . . *Frontispiece*
From a photograph by Marshall in 1875.

"BUT HOW DID IT END?" 52

"YOU SPEAK OF LOVE AND HATE" . 64

THE FIGURE OF THE PARSON SUDDENLY
    TOOK SHAPE 116

DILLINGHAM WATCHED 234

From drawings by Ernest Fosbery.

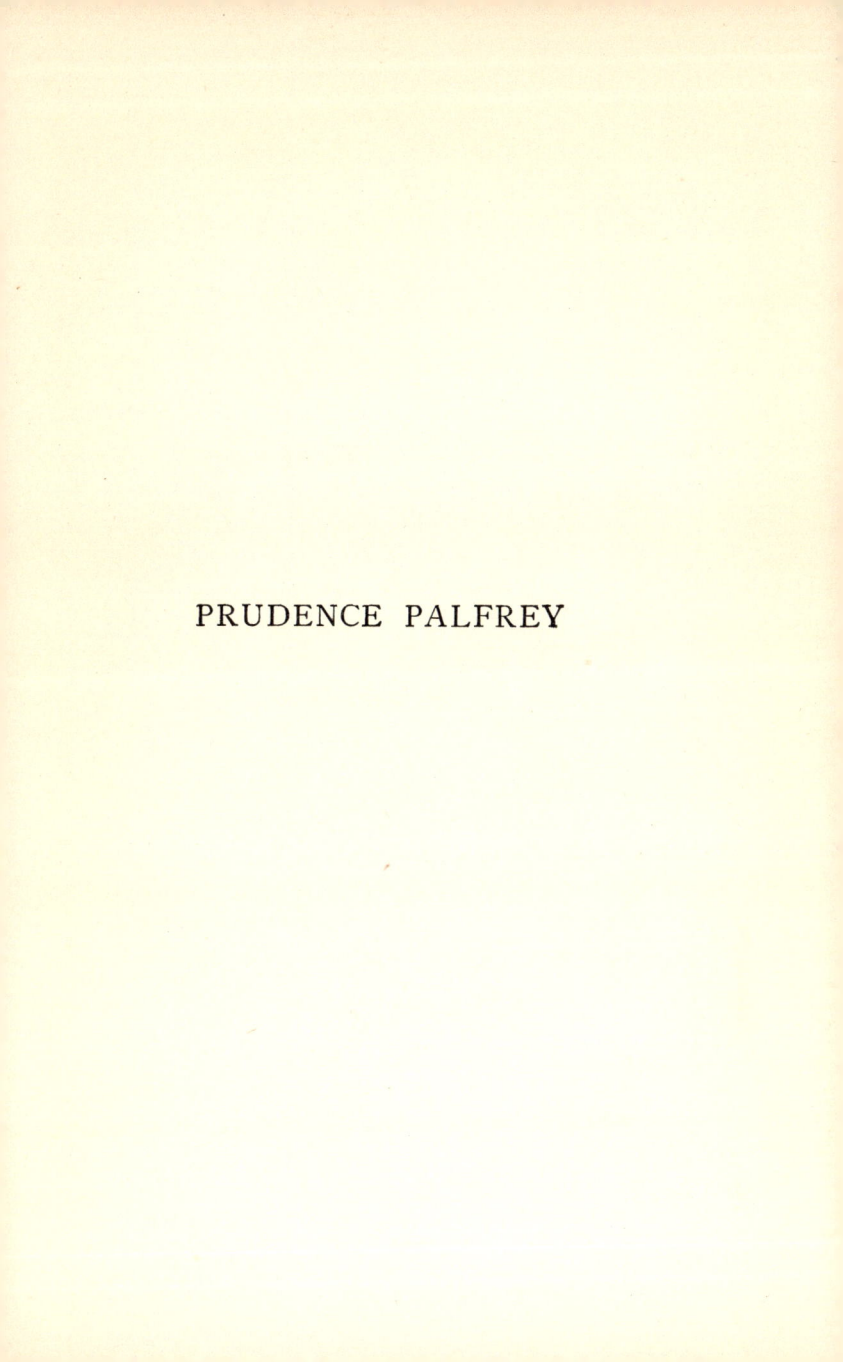

PRUDENCE PALFREY

PRUDENCE PALFREY

I

IN WHICH PARSON WIBIRD HAWKINS RETIRES FROM BUSINESS

Parson Wibird Hawkins was in trouble. The trouble was not of a pecuniary nature, for the good man had not only laid up treasures in heaven, but had kept a temporal eye on the fluctuations of real estate in Rivermouth, and was the owner of three or four of the nicest houses in Hollyhock Row. Nor was his trouble of a domestic nature, whatever it once might have been, for Mrs. Wibird Hawkins was dead this quarter of a century. Nor was it of the kind that sometimes befalls too susceptible shepherds, for the parson had reached an age when the prettiest of his flock might have frisked about him without stirring a pulse.

His trouble was the trouble of all men who, having played their parts nearly if not quite to the end, persist in remaining on the stage to the exclusion of more fiery young actors who have their pieces to speak and their graces to show off. These hapless old men do not perceive that the scene has been changed meanwhile, that twenty or thirty or forty years are supposed to have elapsed; it never occurs to them that they are not the most presentable poets, lunatics, and lovers, until the audience rises up and hoots them, gray hairs and all, from the footlights.

Parson Wibird Hawkins had been prattling innocently to half-averted ears for many a summer and winter. The parish, as a parish, had become tired of old man Hawkins. After fifty years he had begun to pall on them. For fifty years he had christened them and married them and buried them, and held out to them the slightest possible hopes of salvation, in accordance with their own grim theology; and now they wanted to get rid of him, and he never once suspected it — never suspected it, until that day when the deacons waited upon him in his study in the cobwebbed old parsonage, and suggested the expediency of his retirement from active parochial duties. Even then he did not take in the full import of the deacons' communication. Retire from the Lord's vineyard just when his experience was ripest and his heart fullest of his Master's work —

surely they did not mean that! Here he was in his prime, as it were; only seventy-nine last Thanksgiving. He had come among them a young man fresh from the University on the Charles, he had given them the enthusiasm of his youth and the wisdom of his mature manhood, and he would, God willing, continue to labor with them to the end. He would die in the harness. It was his prayer that when the Spirit of the Lord came to take him away, it might find him preaching His word from the pulpit of the Old Brick Church.

"It was very good of you, Deacon Wendell, and you, Deacon Twombly," said the poor old parson, wiping the perspiration from his brow with a large red silk handkerchief dotted with yellow moons; "it was, I must say, very considerate in you to think that I might wish to rest awhile after all these years of labor; but I cannot entertain the idea for a moment."

He had got it into his head that the deacons were proposing a vacation to him, were possibly intending to send him abroad on a tour through Palestine, as the Saint Ann's parish had sent the Rev. Josiah Jones the year before.

"Not," he went on, "but I should like to visit the Holy Land and behold with my own eyes the places made sacred by the footsteps of our Saviour — Jerusalem, and Jordan, and the Mount of Olives — ah! I used to dream of that; but my duties held me here then, and now I cannot bring myself to desert, even temporarily, the flock I have tended so long. Why, I know them all by face and name, and love them all, down to the latest ewe-lamb."

The latest ewe-lamb, by the way, was Deacon Twombly's, and the allusion made him feel very uncomfortable indeed. He glanced uneasily at Deacon Wendell, and Deacon Wendell glanced covertly at him, and they both wished that the duty of dismissing Parson Hawkins had fallen upon somebody else. But the duty was to be performed. The matter had been settled, and the new minister all but decided on, before the deacons went up to the parsonage that afternoon. Even before the king was cold, his subjects had in a manner thrown up their caps for the next in succession. All this had not been brought about, however, without a struggle.

Some of the less progressive members of the parish clung to the ancient order of things. Parson Wibird had been their mainstay in life, sickness, and death for full half a century; they had sprung to manhood and grown gray under his ministrations, and they held it a shame to throw him over now that his voice was a little tremulous and his manner not quite so vigorous as it was. They acknowledged he was not the man he used to be. He wrote no new sermons now; he was turning the barrel upside down, and his latest essay dated back as far as 1850. They admitted it was something of a slip he made, in resurrecting one of those bygone sermons, to allude to General Jackson as "our lately deceased President;" but then the sermon was a good sermon, enough sight better than those sugary discourses without a word of sound doctrine in them, which they had listened to from flibberty-jibberty young ministers from the city. There was one of them the other day — the Sabbath Parson Hawkins was ill — who preached all about somebody named Darwin. Who was Darwin? Darwin was n't one of the Apostles.

"Fur my part," said Mr. Wiggins, the butcher, "I'll be shot ef I don't stan' by the parson. He buried my Merriah Jane fur me, an' I don't fergit it nuther."

As it was notorious that the late Maria Jane had led Mr. Wiggins something of a dance in this life, the unconscious sarcasm of his gratitude caused ill-natured persons to smile.

Uncle Jedd, the sexton of the Old Brick Church, threatened never to dig another grave if they turned off Parson Wibird. Uncle Jedd had a loose idea that such a course on his part would make it rather embarrassing for Rivermouth folks. "Ther' is graves an' ther' is holes," Uncle Jedd would say; "I makes graves, myself, an' I 'm th' only man in th' county thet can."

Unfortunately the parson's supporters constituted the minority, and not an influential minority. The voice of the parish was for the dismissal of the Rev. Wibird Hawkins, and dismissed he should be.

Deacons Wendell and Twombly found their mission perplexing. "We tried to let him down easy, of course," remarked Deacon Zeb Twombly, relating the circumstance afterwards to a group of eager listeners in Odiorne's grocery-store; "but, Lord bless you, you never see an old gentleman so unwillin' and so hard to be let down." The parson persisted in not understanding the drift of the deacons' proposition until, at last, they were forced to use the most explicit language, and in no way soften the blow which they suspected rather than knew would be a heavy one, however adroitly delivered. But when, finally, he was made to comprehend the astounding fact that the Old Brick Church of Rivermouth actually wished him to relinquish his pastorate, then the aged clergyman bowed his head, and, waving his hands in a sort of benediction over the two deacons, retreated slowly, with his chin on his breast, into a little room adjoining the study, leaving the pillars of the church standing rather awkwardly in the middle of the apartment.

II

A PARSON OF THE OLD SCHOOL

Ever since the death of his wife, some twenty-five years previous to the events I am relating, Parson Hawkins had lived in the small house at the foot of Horseshoe Lane. The house stood in the middle of a garden under the shadow of two towering elms, and was so covered by a network of vines, honeysuckle and Virginia creeper, that the oddities of its architecture were not distinctly visible from the street. Though the cottage was not built by the parson, its interior arrangements were as eccentric and inconvenient as if he had designed it. It consisted of three or four one-story Ls which had apparently been added to the main building at various periods, according to the whim or exigency of the occupant. At the right of the hall, which paused abruptly and went up-stairs, so to speak, was the parson's study; opening from this was a smaller chamber, the sanctum sanctorum, lined to the ceiling with theological works; and beyond this again, though not communicating with it, was the room where the parson slept. At the left of the hall was the parlor, redolent of mahogany furniture and the branches of pungent spruce which choked the wide chimney-place summer and winter, for the parlor was seldom used. Then came the dining-room, and next to that the kitchen. Leading from the former were two sleeping-chambers, one occupied by Salome Pinder, the parson's housekeeper. The second story of the main building had been left unfinished on the inside. Viewed from the garden gate, the zigzag roofs, touched here and there with patches of purple and gold moss, presented the appearance of a collection of military cocked hats.

It was altogether a grotesque, ruinous, tumbledown place, and people wondered why Parson Hawkins should have given up his stately house on Pleasant Street and moved to Horseshoe Lane, and why he remained there. But Salome Pinder understood it.

"The parson, you see," said Salome, "is gittin' a leetle near in his old age. He 'pears to git nearer an' nearer ev'ry year. When Mis' Hawkins was alive, why, bless you! there was n't nothin' too handsum nor expen*sive* for her, an' I won't say she was over an' above grateful, for she was n't ; but she 's dead, the poor creeter, an' the best of us lack more 'n wings to be angils. The day after the funeral the parson says, 'S'lome,' says he, 'we 'll move into the cottage, it 's quite good enough for me.' 'Nothin' 's too good for you, Parson Wibird,' says I. But he did n't feel content in the great house, an' it was sort o' lonely; so move we did, to the disapp'intment of some — I don't mention no names — who thought that mebbe the parson would invite 'em up to Pleasant Street permanent. P'rhaps the Widder Mugridge was the most disapp'inted. But, Lord love you, the parson ain't one of them that is always runnin' after wimmin folks. He 's ben married onest."

That was very true, and that Parson Hawkins's matrimonial venture was not altogether of an encouraging complexion seems likely; for he declined to repeat the experiment. For several years after the translation of Mrs. Hawkins, the parish supposed he would take another helpmeet, and, in fact, more than one seductive cap had been sedately set for him; but the parson had shown himself strangely obtuse. He was not an old man at that time, but he loved quiet, and perhaps his life had not been too tranquil under Mrs. Hawkins's reign. Besides, as Salome said, the parson was becoming a little near, not in a general

PRUDENCE PALFREY

way, but in his personal expenses. The poor knew how broad and practical his charity was. His closeness manifested itself only in matters pertaining to his own comfort. He seemed to regard himself as an unworthy and designing person, who was obtaining food and clothes under false pretences from Parson Hawkins.

These economical tendencies had flowered out occasionally in his wife's time, but had been promptly taken up by the roots. Whenever his coat showed signs of wear or his hat became a trifle dilapidated, Mrs. Hawkins had made him buy a new one. It was whispered in and out of the parish that once, when the parson protested against replenishing his wardrobe, Mrs. Hawkins, who appears to have been a person of considerable executive ability, settled the question by putting the parson's best waistcoat in the kitchen fire. I do not vouch for the truth of the story, for, though nothing occurs in Rivermouth without being known, a great many things are known there that never occur at all.

This may have been one of them ; but it is certain that after Parson Hawkins took up his abode in the small house he neglected himself frightfully. His linen was always scrupulously neat and fresh, for Salome saw to that ; but he wore his coats until the seams stood out pathetically, like the bones of the late Mr. Jamison, the Living Skeleton, who used to travel with Van Amburgh's Circus, and must have given Death very little trouble to make a ghost of him. Of course Salome could not put the old gentleman's coats into the kitchen stove when they became shabby. The parson's thriftiness increased with his years, and no doubt sorely cramped Salome, who had a New England housewife's appreciation of bountiful living, and to whom a riotous number of mince-pies was a necessity at Thanksgiving. She uttered no complaint, however, and was quick to resent any reflection on her master's domestic parsimony.

"We could live on the fat of the land if we wanted to," said Salome to Mrs. Waldron, who had dropped in of an afternoon to gossip. "The parson he's a rich man as time goes, an' the pore oughter be thankful for it. He feeds the widder an' the fatherless, instead of a-stuffin' hisself."

"I wanter know, now!"

Salome's homely statement was strictly accurate. However severe the internal economy at the small house in Horseshoe Lane, the poor were not scrimped. The Widow Pepperell had her winter fuel regularly; and the two Clemmer boys, whose father had leaned against a circular saw in the Miantonomoh Mills, knew precisely where their winter jackets were coming from. Even wayside tramps — there were no professional mendicants in Rivermouth — halted instinctively at the modest white gate. Doubtless the parson helped many a transparent impostor on his winding way. There was a certain yellow dog that used to walk lame up to the scullery door for a bone, and then run away with it very nimbly on four legs. Sandy Marden's Skye-terrier was likely enough only a fair type of many that shared the parson's bounty.

He had been a prosperous man. When he first came to Rivermouth he purchased a lot of land at the west end of the town, as a pasture for a horse which he neglected or forgot to buy. The "minister's pasture" became a standing joke. It turned out a very excellent joke in the end. Several times he was tempted to sell the land for less than he gave for it; but it had cost him little, and he thought that perhaps it might be worth something more by and by; so he held on to it. As the town grew, fashion drifted in that direction. Then Captain Pendexter put up his haughty Gothic mansion at the head of Anchor Street. That settled the business. A colony of French-roof houses sprang up as if by magic along Josselyn

Avenue, and the "minister's pasture" was about as valuable a piece of property as there was in Rivermouth. So it came to pass that Parson Hawkins was a moderately rich man. The people thought the parson was pretty shrewd, when perhaps he was only pretty lucky: if he had been shrewd he would have sold the land long before it was worth anything. Another speculation he entered into at this time was not so successful. If the local tradition is correct, Colonel Trueworthy Dennett's daughter Dorcas got the best of that bargain.

But for many years now the parson's lines had fallen in pleasant places. The tumult and jar of life never reached him among his books in the twelve-by-nine library in Horseshoe Lane. The fateful waves of time and chance that beat about the world surged and broke far away from the little garden with its bright row of sentinel hollyhocks and its annual encampments of marigolds and nasturtiums. To be sure he had had, four or five years before this chronicle opens, what he regarded as a grievous affliction. The parish, contrary to his wishes, had removed the old pine-wood pulpit and replaced it with an ornate new-fangled black-walnut affair thick with grotesque carvings like a heathen idol. The old pulpit was hallowed by

PRUDENCE PALFREY

a hundred associations; it had been built in King George's time; eminent divines whose names are fresh in our colonial history had stood under that antiquated sounding-board; but, after all, what did it matter to him whether he expounded the Scriptures from pine or black walnut, so long as he was permitted to teach his children the way and the life? His annoyance was but transient, and he came to look upon it as a vanity and vexation of spirit on his part. But now a real trouble had come to him.

While the two deacons were engaged with the parson in the study that May afternoon, Salome Pinder moved about the hall and the dining-room with strange restlessness. Few things went on in the cottage without her cognizance. Not that Salome was given to eavesdropping; but the rooms were contracted, the partitions thin, and words spoken in even the usual conversational tone had a trick of repeating themselves in the adjacent apartments. The study door was ajar, and Salome could scarcely help catching scraps of the dialogue from time to time.

Long before the deacons took their departure she knew very well what had happened. In fact, when she saw Deacon Twombly and Deacon Wendell coming up the garden walk, she felt their visit to be ominous. Salome knew of the dissatisfaction that had been brewing in the parish for months past. That Parson Hawkins never dreamed of it shows how unfitted he was to serve longer. The appearance of the executioners, with warrant and bow-string, was the first intimation he had of his downfall.

Salome was appalled by what had taken place, though in a degree prepared for it. She was so flustered that she neglected to open the front door for the retreating deacons, but left them, as the parson had done, to find their way out as best they might.

It was some time before she could gather strength to cross the hall and look into the study. The parson was not there; he was in the little inner room, and the door was locked. Salome tried the latch and spoke to him several times without getting a reply. Then the parson told her gently to go away, he was engaged, he would talk with her presently. But Salome did not go away; she sunk into a chair and sat there with her hands folded listlessly in her lap — a more abject figure, perhaps, than the old parson on the other side of the door.

The scent of the lilacs came in at the open window, and the leaves of the vines trailing over the casement outside made wavering silhouettes on the uncarpeted floor of the study. The robins sang full-throated in the garden, as if there were no such thing in the world as care. Salome listened, and wondered vaguely at their merriment.

The afternoon sunlight slipped from the eaves and the shadows deepened under the great elms. The phantom leaves at Salome's feet had vanished ; the songs of the robins had died away to faint and intermittent twitterings, and the early twilight crept into the study. Now and then she fancied she heard the parson moving in the little room ; he seemed to be walking to and fro at intervals, like some poor caged animal. She could not tell.

It was nearly dark when the garden gate swung to with a sharp click, and a quick, light footstep sounded on the gravel walk. Salome rose hastily from the chair, and reached the street-door just as some one stepped upon the porch.

It was a girl of nineteen or twenty, but looking younger with her hair blown about her brows by the fresh May wind. She held in one hand a chip-straw hat which had slipped from its place, and with the other was pushing back an enviable mass of brown hair, showing a serious, pale face, a little flushed at the cheeks with walking. It was a face which, passing it heedlessly in the street, you would be likely to retain in your memory unconsciously. The wide gray eyes, capable of great tenderness and great haughtiness, would come back to you vividly, may be, years afterwards. The girl was not a beauty in the ordinary sense, but she had what some one has described as a haunting face. Who has not caught a chance expression on some face in a crowd — a lifting of the eye, a turn of the lip, an instantaneous revelation of strength or weakness — and never forgotten it? I have a fancy, which I do not thrust upon the reader, that the person who casts this spell on us would exert a marked influence over our destiny if circumstance brought us in contact with him or her. He or she would be our good angel or our evil star.

As the girl stood there now on the porch, she looked little enough like playing the part of a Fate. With her heavy hair blown in clouds over her eyes, she looked rather like a Shetland pony.

"O Miss Prue! is that you, honey?" cried Salome. "Do jest step in an' speak to the parson; he's in a peck of trouble."

"I was afraid so, Salome. Where is he?" asked the girl, pushing open the door of the study and seeing it unoccupied.

PRUDENCE PALFREY

"He's locked hisself in the sanctrum," whispered Salome.

"Locked himself in?"

"Yes, an' there he's ben ever sence them plaguy deacons went away, more 'n two hours."

"May be he will not care to see me just now, Salome?"

"Mebbe — dunno; but do jest speak a word to him."

"If you think I had better?"

"I do, honey."

"How strange — to lock himself in!"

Then Prudence Palfrey crossed the study, and tapped softly on the panel of the inner door.

III

MR. DENT AND HIS WARD

AND there we must leave her, with uplifted hand and listening ear, while the reader is made acquainted with the personages who figure in this little drama, and is put into possession of certain facts necessary to a clear understanding of it.

Among those who had been instrumental in removing Parson Hawkins from the pastorate of the Brick Church was Mr. Ralph Dent, a retired brewer of considerable wealth and much local influence. He was not, as a general thing, deeply concerned in parish affairs; he contributed liberally to every worthy charitable project, and was always to be seen in his pew at the morning service; but it was of comparatively small moment to him whether the parson's discourse was long or short, brilliant or dull, for he invariably went to sleep. Mr. Dent, for reasons which will appear, did not admire Parson Hawkins warmly; but if Mr. Dent had loved him he would have gone to sleep all the same. There are men who cannot, to save themselves from perdition, keep awake in sermon-time.

So Mr. Dent had no objection to Parson Hawkins as a parson; but he was aware that many in the parish had rather strong objections. The congregation embraced a large number of young persons, chiefly women, who always like their minister sleek and interesting, and they were not content with what had satisfied their grandparents. The old pastor was visibly breaking up, and a new man was wanted. Now it chanced that Mr. Dent, in one of his periodical visits to New York, had made the acquaintance of a Mr. James Dillingham, a young gentleman of fortune and aristocratic Southern connections, who was travelling in the North for his health. Mr. Dillingham had been educated for the ministry, but, owing to ill health, and perhaps to his passion for travel, had never been settled permanently over a society. A quick friendship sprung up between the two men, despite the disparity of their years, for Mr. Dillingham was not more than twenty-eight, and Mr. Dent was well on in the second half of that ridiculously brief term allotted to moderns. In the course of various conversations, Mr. Dillingham became interested in Rivermouth, and thought that perhaps he would visit the lovely New England seaport before returning South. He would certainly do so, if he undertook his proposed pilgrimage to Quebec. But the Canadian tour and even his return South were involved in considerable uncertainty. The bombardment of Fort Sumter by the South Carolinians had brought matters to a crisis; war was inevitable. Mr. Dillingham's property was largely invested in Western and Northern securities, fortunately for him; for, though he was Southern born and bred, he had no sympathy with the disunionists of his native State. In the meantime it might be necessary for him to make the North his home.

It flashed on Mr. Dent that here was the very man for the Old Brick Church. Young, wealthy, in good social position, and of unusually winning address, he would be a notable acquisition to Rivermouth society. He broached the subject indirectly to his friend, who was not at first disposed to discuss it as a possibility; then Mr. Dent urged the matter warmly, and had nearly carried his point, when he was obliged to go back to Rivermouth.

At Rivermouth he laid the case before the deacons; they opened a correspondence with Mr. Dillingham, which resulted in his agreement to preach for them on the last Sunday in

May following. "Then," he wrote, "we shall be in a position to decide on the best course, should the vacancy occur to which you allude in your letter." This was satisfactory. Mr. Dillingham was not to be drawn into an inconsiderate engagement. But then Mr. Dillingham was rich, and not like those poor, drowning clergymen, dragged down by large families, ready to clutch at such frail straws of salary as Rivermouth could hold out. Upon this it was decided to relieve Parson Hawkins of his charge, and take the chances of securing Mr. Dillingham.

Throughout the matter Mr. Dent had acted on impulse, as the most practical man sometimes will, and had been in no way swayed by personal animosity towards Parson Hawkins, for he felt none. But when all was said and done, a misgiving shot across him. What would Prue say? She all but worshipped the old parson. Mr. Dent himself, as I have more than intimated, did not worship the parson. There had been an occasion, a painful passage in Prue's life, when it seemed to Mr. Dent that Parson Hawkins had stood between him and the girl. All that was past and nearly forgotten now; but the time had been when he thought the minister was alienating Prue's affections from him.

Prudence Palfrey was Mr. Dent's ward. His guardianship had a certain tinge of romance to it, though perhaps no man was less romantic than Mr. Dent. He was a straightforward, practical man, naturally amiable and accidentally peppery, who had had his living to make, and had made it by making beer. A romantic brewer would be an anomaly. There is something essentially prosaic in vats and barrels; but this did not restrain Mr. Dent in early life from falling in love with Mercy Gardner — for brewers are human, though they may not be poetical — nor is it likely that the brewery, which was then a flourishing establishment, had anything to do with her refusal to marry him. She married his bookkeeper, Edward Palfrey, and went to the Bermudas, where Palfrey had obtained a clerkship in an English house. There, after five years, he fell a victim to an epidemic, and the widow, with her three-year-old girl, drifted back to Rivermouth. Dent bore a constant mind, and would probably have married his old love, but Mrs. Palfrey died suddenly, leaving Prudence and what small property there was to his charge.

He had been faithful to the trust, and had had his reward. The pretty ways and laughter of the child had been pleasant in his lonely home, for he never married. Then the straight, slim girl, looking at him with Mercy Gardner's eyes and speaking to him with Mercy Gardner's voice, had nearly consoled him for all; and now the bloom of her womanhood filled his house with subtile light and beauty. In all his plans Prue's interest was the end. Whatever tenderness there was in his nature turned itself towards her. For her sake he acquired a knowledge of books, and became an insatiable reader, as men always do who take to books late in life. He sold out the brewery, not so much because he was tired of it as that he did not want the townsfolk to be able to say that Prudence Palfrey was only the brewer's girl. When she was of age to go into society, the best houses in town were open to Mr. Dent and his ward — the Goldstones', the Blydenburghs', and the Grimes's — which might not have been the case if the old brewery had not faded into the dim and blessed past.

It must be understood that there are circles in Rivermouth into which a brewer in the present tense could no more penetrate than a particularly fat camel could go through the eye of a remarkably fine cambric needle — charmed circles, where the atmosphere is so rarefied that after you have got into it the best thing you can do, perhaps, is to get out of it again.

It is not well to analyze the thing closely. It is all a mystery. One is pained to find that the most exclusive persons have frequently passed their early manhood in selling tape or West India groceries in homœopathic quantities. This is not an immoral thing in itself, but it is certainly illogical in these persons to be so intolerent of those less fortunate folks who have not yet disposed of their stock. However, this is much too vast and gloomy a subject for my narrow canvas.

Mr. Dent was proud of social position for Prue's sake. There was no girl like her in Rockingham County. When he bought Willowbrook, a spacious house with grounds and outbuildings, a mile from the town, she sat at the head of his table like a lady as she was, for she had honest New England blood in her veins. That Prudence was as dear to him as if she had been his own daughter, he fully believed; but how completely she had curled about his heart, like a vine, he did not discover until his nephew, John Dent, fell in love with her and all but married her out of hand. This must also be told while Prue is kept waiting at the parson's study door.

IV

DRAGONS

When Prudence was turning eighteen — that is to say, nearly three years before that afternoon in May when she is introduced to the reader — John Dent had come to Rivermouth. He had recently graduated, with not too many honors, and was taking a breathing-spell previous to setting out on his adventures in the world; for he had his dragons to overcome and his spurs to win, like any young knight in a legend. Poverty and Inexperience, among the rest, are very formidable dragons. They slay more young men every year than are ever heard of. The stripling knight, with his valise neatly packed by the tearful baroness, his mother, sallies forth in a spick-and-span new armor from the paternal castle — and, snap! that is the last of him. Now and then one comes back with gold-pieces and decorations, but, ah! for the numbers that go down before the walls of great towns like New York and Boston and Chicago!

John Dent's family had formerly lived in Rivermouth, where he had lost his mother in infancy. At this time his father was associated in the proprietorship of the brewery, from which he subsequently withdrew to engage in some Western railroad enterprise. When Mr. Benjamin Dent moved to Illinois, John was a mere child; he had not been in Rivermouth since; his vacations had been passed with his father, and he had only the vaguest memory of his childhood's home. It was a cherished memory, nevertheless; for an unwavering affection for the place of one's nativity seems to be one of the conditions of birth in New England. It was during John Dent's last term in college that his father had died, leaving his railroad affairs hopelessly complicated. Though communication between the two brothers had been infrequent of late years, the warmest feeling had existed on both sides, and Mr. Ralph Dent was eager with purse and advice to assist his nephew in any business or profession he might select.

John Dent was quite undecided what to do with himself. When some outlying personal debts were paid off there would be enough left to keep him afloat a year. Within that year of course he must have his plans definitely settled. He had come to Rivermouth to talk over those plans with his uncle, and a room had been provided for him at Willowbrook.

"Look here, Prue," Mr. Dent had said, laughingly, the day his nephew was expected, "I won't have you making eyes at him."

"But I will, though!" Prudence had cried, glancing back over her shoulder, "if he is anything like his uncle."

But John Dent did not resemble his uncle, and Prue did not make eyes at him. She found him very agreeable, nevertheless, a tall, frank-hearted young fellow with dark hair and alert black eyes — in every way different from the abstracted young student her fancy had taken the liberty to paint for her. He smoked his uncle's cabañas as if he had been born to them, and amused Prue vastly with descriptions of his college life and with the funny little profiles of his college chums which he drew on blotting-paper in the library. If he could have been examined in caricature or allowed to graduate from the gymnasium, he would not have come off so poorly for honors.

Prudence had rather dreaded the advent of the gloomy scholastic, and had been rather curious about him also. They had played together at a period when Prue was a little child and John Dent wore pinafores. They had not met since then. It was odd for her old playfellow to be an utter stranger to her now. What sort of man was that little boy whom she had lost so long ago in the misty fairyland of babyhood? A solemn young man in black, she had fancied. She had pictured him prowling about the house and lawn, brooding like the young Prince of Denmark, not on psychological subtleties indeed, but on sordid questions as to how on earth he was going to get his living. How he was going to get his living did not seem to trouble John Dent in the least.

Reading one of Thackeray's novels in a hammock on the piazza, or strolling in the garden after supper, with his cigar glowing here and there among the shrubbery like a panther's eye, he did not appear much appalled by prospective struggles for existence. The Dents were always that way, Mr. Ralph Dent remarked; free and easy, with lots of latent energy. Put a Dent in a desert, and he would directly build some kind of a manufactory. A brewery likely enough.

And indeed there was something under John Dent's careless manner which seemed to give the assurance that when the time arrived he would overthrow the wicked giants and slay the enchanted dragons with neatness and despatch, like a brave modern knight in an English walking-coat and a mauve silk neckerchief drawn through an amethyst ring. Uncle Ralph thought there was a good deal to the boy — and so did Prue.

He was superior to any young man she had ever seen. She had seen few, to be sure, for Rivermouth is a sterile spot in which to pick up a sustenance, and her young male eagles generally fly from the nest as soon as they are fledged, some seaward and others to the neighboring inland cities. They are mostly sickly eagles that are left. So Prudence had encountered few young men in her time, and those she had not liked; but she did like John Dent.

John Dent had come to Rivermouth bearing about his person some concealed wounds inflicted by the eldest daughter of his Greek professor; he had, in fact, been "stabbed with a white wench's black eye, shot through the ear with a love-song," as Mercutio phrases it; but before ten days were gone at Willowbrook these wounds had somehow healed over, leaving scarcely a cicatrice on his memory.

Given a country-house, with a lawn and a pine grove, and two young persons with nothing in the world to do — let the season be springtime or winter — and it requires no wizard to tell the result. Prue, with her genuine fresh nature and trim figure and rich hair and gray eyes, was easy to like, and very much easier to love. I am not trying to find reasons for these young persons. If people who pair were obliged to have good reasons for pairing, there would be a falling off in the census.

It came to pass, then, at the end of four weeks, that John Dent found himself thinking night and day of his uncle's ward. He knew it was a hopeless thing from the start. He was twenty-three, penniless, and without a profession. Nothing was less tenable than the idea that his uncle would permit Prudence to engage herself to a man who might not be in a position these five years to give her a home. Then as to Prudence herself, he had no grounds for assuming that she cared for him. She had been very frank and pleasant, as was permissible to the nephew of her guardian; her conduct had been from the beginning without a shadow of coquetry. She had made no eyes at him.

Prudence would not have been a woman and eighteen if she had not seen somewhat how matters were going with the young gentleman. She did not love him, as yet; but she liked him more than any one she had ever known. She knew as well as he that anything beyond friendship between them would be unfortunate.

She determined to afford him no opportunity to speak to her of love, if he were so unwise. She would keep him at such a distance as would render it difficult for him to indulge in the slightest sentiment with her. Prue had passed to her eighteenth birthday without so much as a flirtation; but she at once set to work managing John Dent with the cool skill of a seaside belle in her second season. It is so a young duck takes to water.

There were no moonlight walks on the lawn any more; but it fell out so naturally that John Dent saw no diplomacy in it. Household duties, which she could have no hand in conjuring, rose up between them and the pine grove. People from the town, very stupid people, dropped into the drawing-room of an evening, or his uncle failed to drop out. When they were alone together, and frequently when Mr. Dent was present, Prudence would rally the young man about the professor's daughter whom he had mentioned incidentally early in his visit. She suspected a tenderness in that direction, and in handling the subject developed powers of sarcasm quite surprising to herself. She was full of liveliness those days.

John Dent was not lively now; he was gradually merging into that saturnine and melancholy-eyed student whom Prue had so dreaded.

Mr. Ralph Dent was struck by this phenomenon. It seemed to him latterly that his ward laughed too much and his nephew not enough. It had been the other way. Mr. Dent was, as I have said, a practical man, except in this, that he expected other persons to be practical. He did not dream that his nephew would have the audacity to fall in love with Prue. But the change that had come over the two gave Mr. Dent a twinge of uneasiness. Perhaps he had not been wholly wise in having John Dent at Willowbrook.

The more he reflected on Prue's high spirits and his nephew's sudden low ones, the less he admired it. If there had been any nonsense between them, he would put a stop to it before it went any further.

Running through the Willowbrook grounds was a winding rivulet spanned by a rustic bridge, at the farther end of which, under a clump of willows, stood a summer-house — an octagon-shaped piece of lattice-work with four gilt balls suspended from a little blue spire on the roof: a Yankee's idea of a pagoda. Here John Dent was thoughtfully smoking a cigar one morning when he saw his uncle cross the birch-wood bridge and come towards him. Mr.

Dent stepped into the summer-house, seated himself opposite the young man, took out his cigar-case, and went directly to the business in hand.

"Jack," said Mr. Dent, "I hope you have n't been talking any nonsense to Prue."

"I don't think I understand you," said Jack, with a little start. "I have n't, to my knowledge, been talking any nonsense to her."

"For the last week or so you have not seemed like yourself, and I fancied that perhaps something had happened between you and Prue — a little tiff may be."

"Nothing in the world, sir."

Mr. Dent, like Hamlet, wanted something "more relative than this."

"You are sure you have not been making love to her, Jack?"

"I have certainly not been making love to Miss Palfrey, if that is what you mean."

Mr. Dent drew a breath of relief. If his nephew had one trait stronger than another, it was truthfulness. Mr. Dent was satisfied that no mischief had been done so far, and he intended to preclude the possibility of mischief. "How stupid of me," he reflected, "to put the notion into the fellow's head!" He would cover his maladroit move by getting his nephew into a New York banking-house or an insurance office at once. The sooner Jack made a start in life the better. Mr. Dent bit off the end of his cigar, and, taking a light from the young man, said, "Of course, Jack, I did n't seriously think you had."

With this he rose and was about to leave the summer-house.

"Are you going to town, uncle?" inquired John Dent, looking up.

"Yes."

"I'll walk a bit of the way with you, if you like."

"Certainly, Jack."

As the garden gate closed on uncle and nephew, Prudence looked out of the bay-window over the hall door, and her busy, intelligent needle came to a dead halt halfway through a piece of cambric muslin. She was aware that her guardian was going to town; but it was not one of John Dent's habits to take long walks with his uncle. Prue pondered the circumstance for a minute or so, and then the needle went on again as busily as before.

"Uncle Ralph," said John Dent, as they reached a rise of ground overlooking the spires and gables of Rivermouth and the picturesque harbor, where a man-of-war lay at anchor with its masts and spars black against the sparkling atmosphere, "I had half resolved to say something to you this morning, but after your question in the summer-house I feel it my duty to say it."

"What is that, Jack?"

"I told you I had not been making love to Miss Palfrey, but I am bound to tell you that I love her all the same."

"What! why, I never heard of such madness!" And Mr. Dent stopped short in the middle of the road.

"I did n't suppose it would meet with your approval, sir."

"My approval? I tell you I never heard of such insanity!"

"I know it is unfortunate," said John Dent humbly; "but there are things which no man can help."

"But a man should help falling in love with a girl when he is not able to provide birdseed for a canary."

"The birdseed will come in good time; it always does."

Mr. Dent's glance, by the merest accident, rested on the red-brick Almshouse which loomed up on the left. John Dent followed his glance, and colored.

"Do you expect a young woman to waste the bloom of her life waiting for you, and finally go with you over there?"

"The girl who will not wait a year or two, or ten years, for the man she loves, is not worth working for," said John Dent, nettled.

Then Mr. Dent cursed himself for his blindness in bringing these two together.

"And Prue loves you?" he gasped.

"I didn't say that, sir."

"What in the devil did you say, then?"

"I said I loved her. I think she doesn't care a straw for me."

"But you spoke of her waiting for you a year or two."

"That was merely a supposititious case."

"Have you hinted anything of this to Prue?"

"No, sir."

"Then I depend on your honor not to. I won't have it! I won't have it!" And Mr. Dent stood there quite white with anger.

"You will bear in mind, Uncle Ralph, that I need not have told you this."

"That would have been dishonorable."

"It would have been dishonorable, sir; and so I came to you directly, without breathing a word to Miss Palfrey. I did not forget I was under your roof."

Certainly John Dent had not been dishonorable, however mad. Mr. Dent knew that his nephew was wrong in falling in love with his ward, and that he himself was right in being indignant; yet he was conscious that his young kinsman had in a fashion disarmed him.

"This is exceedingly awkward," he said, after a silence. "I was very glad to have you at Willowbrook, but with this extraordinary avowal" —

John Dent interrupted him: "Of course my visit is at an end. I knew that. I shall leave to-day."

"What are your plans?"

"I have none, that is, nothing definite."

"I mean, where are you going?"

"Oh, I shall take a room somewhere in the town for the present."

Mr. Dent did not like that. The nice sense of honor which had sealed the young man's lips while beneath the avuncular roof might take wing under different circumstances. Rivermouth was a strong strategical position from which to lay siege to Willowbrook. Mr. Dent did not like that at all.

"Why waste your time in Rivermouth? There is no opening for you there. Why not go to Boston, or better still, to New York" (or to Jericho, Mr. Dent interpolated mentally), "where there are countless chances for a young man like you?"

"I can live more economically in the town.

Besides, I do not intend to settle in any of our Eastern cities. I shall go to some new country where there are wider and less crowded fields for enterprise, where fortunes are made rapidly. I wish to make my pile at once."

"Quite a unique case," Mr. Dent could not refrain from remarking.

"Then," continued John Dent, shedding the sarcasm placidly, "I shall come back and ask Miss Palfrey to be my wife, if her heart and hand are free."

"You will do me the favor to delay the question until you come back," cried Mr. Dent, whose wrath was fanned into flame again. "If you insist on idling about Rivermouth, I insist on your promise that you will not explain your views to Miss Palfrey."

"I will not make any promises," returned John Dent, "because I have an unfortunate habit of keeping them."

Was it possible that Prue was tangled, even ever so slightly, in the meshes of the same net that had caught this luckless devil-fish? After his nephew's confession, Mr. Dent was prepared for almost anything.

Mr. Dent said: "But unless you do give me some such assurance, I shall be constrained to forbid your visits to the house, and that would cause people to talk."

"Even with that alternative, I cannot make you any promise. To be candid, I have n't at this moment the faintest intention of telling Miss Palfrey what my sentiments are. It is not likely I shall see her again, since you have walled up the doors of Willowbrook," he added, with a smile. "Uncle Ralph, let us talk sense."

"Thanks for the compliment implied."

"Don't mention it," said Jack politely.

"Look here," said Mr. Dent, resting his hand on his young kinsman's shoulder, "I do not want to shut my doors on you. It annoys me beyond measure to have my brother Ben's boy flying in the face of reason in this way, and setting himself up in antagonism to me, his best friend. Come, now, Jack, don't be a simpleton. Go to New York, look up some business or profession to your taste, and you shall have any capital you require, if you will give over this foolishness about Prue."

"I could not do it, Uncle Ralph. I love her."

He had said that before quietly enough. The words were spoken passionately this time, and they went through Mr. Dent's heart with inexplicable sharpness.

"I love her, and I should despise myself if I could be bought. All the chances are against me, I know; but if I cannot have her, I can at least try to be worthy of her."

"Stuff and nonsense! How many girls have you fallen in love with before now?"

"Seven or eight, first and last, as nearly as I can remember," replied young Dent candidly; "but there was no Prudence Palfrey among them. I think that when a man loves a girl like her, he loves but once."

"All this comes of your verse-writing and moonshine. I don't know where you got them from. Your father was a plain, practical man, and kept his head cool. When I was a young fellow" —

"You fell in love with Mercy Gardner," cried John Dent, "and never loved any but her."

Mr. Dent winced a little as he parried the thrust.

"But I could not have her, and I made the best of it, like a sensible man. You cannot have her daughter, and you are making the worst of it, like an obstinate fellow."

"But I am not sure I cannot have the daughter — some time."

"I tell you so."

John Dent decapitated a thistle with one impatient stroke of his cane. Off came his uncle's head — by proxy!

PRUDENCE PALFREY 45

"When Miss Palfrey tells me with her own lips to go about my business, then it will be time enough for me to draw on those stores of philosophy and hard common sense which are supposed to be handed down in the Dent family."

Mr. Dent's anger flashed out at that, and it must be owned his nephew was exasperating.

"I command you never to speak to her of this!"

"But I must, one of these days."

"You refuse positively to quit Rivermouth?"

"At present I do."

"And you will make no promise relative to Miss Palfrey?"

"I cannot do that, either, sir."

"Then you cannot call at the house, you know," cried Mr. Dent. "I forbid you to speak to her when you meet her, on the street or elsewhere, and I'll have nothing to do with you from this out!"

And Mr. Dent turned on his heel and walked rapidly down the road in the direction of Willowbrook, forgetful of those two ounces and a half of scarlet Saxony wool which he had been commissioned by Prue to purchase at Rivermouth.

"'How poor are they that have not patience'!" said the young man to himself; then he added, a second after, "How poor are they that have not prudence!" probably meaning Prudence Palfrey.

John Dent looked at his cigar. It had gone out. He threw the stump among some barberry-bushes by the stone wall, and set his face towards the town.

V

THE ROMANCE OF HORSESHOE LANE

JOHN DENT did not return to Willowbrook to dinner. The meal was passed in unwonted silence. Mr. Dent was preoccupied, and Prudence was conscious of something in the atmosphere inimical to conversation. Once or twice her guardian looked up from his plate as if to address her, and then seemed to change his mind.

"Where is Cousin John?" at last asked Prudence, setting the almonds and raisins nearer to Mr. Dent.

"Oh, by the way, I forgot to say he was not coming to dinner! He — he dines in town."

"At the Blydenburghs'?"

There was a certain Miss Veronica Blydenburgh, and a very pretty girl, let me tell you.

"I don't know. How should I know?" replied Mr. Dent crisply.

"Will he return to tea?" ventured Prudence, after a pause.

"I don't think he will," Mr. Dent said, pushing back his chair. "In fact, I do not think he will return here at all; he has some matters in town requiring his attention for a few days, and then he is off. He sent good-by to you," added Mr. Dent, committing a little amiable perjury in the attempt to rob his nephew's sudden departure of its brusqueness.

Then Mr. Dent walked out of the dining-room.

"Not coming back at all, and sent good-by to me!" said Prudence to herself. "Assuredly, Cousin John has not strained many points to be polite, after being our guest for six weeks."

Then she recalled the walk which Cousin John had taken with his uncle in the morning; she put this and that together, and became contemplative.

As Prudence and her guardian were sitting on the piazza an hour or two later, Clem Hoyt, the local Mercury and expressman, drove up to the gate with an order for Mr. J. Dent's trunk, and an unsealed note for Miss Palfrey which Mr. Dent handed to her with an indescribable grimace.

The writer expressed his regret at not being able to say his adieux to her in person; he had been called away unexpectedly; he would never forget her kindness to him during the past six weeks, but would always be her very faithful cousin John Dent. That was all.

Prudence turned the paper over and over, and upside down, to see if a postscript had not escaped her; but that was the whole of it. It was almost as telegrammatic as the royal epistle to the queen in Ruy Blas — *Madam, the wind is high, and I have killed six wolves.*

"Uncle Ralph," said Prue, folding up the note and slipping it back into the envelope, "I know that something unpleasant has happened."

"What does he say?"

"He? — nothing. But something has happened."

Mr. Dent tilted back his chair and made no rejoinder.

"What is it? Have you quarrelled with him?"

"We did have a misunderstanding."

"What about, uncle?"

"About money matters chiefly."

"If it was all about money," said Prudence, "I have no business to ask questions."

"The boy made a fool of himself generally," returned Mr. Dent incautiously.

"Then it was not money chiefly?" said

Prudence, walking up to him and looking into his eyes. "Uncle Ralph, was it anything connected with me?"

"Prue, my dear, I would rather not discuss the subject."

"But, uncle, if it was about me, I ought to know it. It would make me very unhappy to be the cause of dissension between you and your nephew, and not know what I have done. I might keep on doing it all the time, you know."

"You haven't done anything, child; it is Jack's doing."

"*What* is Jack's doing?"

"Since you will have it, I suppose I must tell you."

But Mr. Dent was at a loss how to tell her, and hesitated. Should he treat the affair lightly or seriously? The idea of Prue having a lover was both comical and alarming to him.

"Well, what did Cousin John do?"

"He did me the honor, this morning, to say that he was in love with you — did you ever hear anything so absurd?"

Prudence opened her eyes wide.

"Well?"

"Well? Well, I thought it rather absurd myself."

"That anybody should love me?" said Prue slyly.

"Not at all; but that Jack should allow himself to be interested in any one under the circumstances. I pointed out to him the mistake of his even dreaming of marriage in his present position. What folly! Setting you entirely aside, what could Jack do with a wife? She would be a millstone tied to his neck. Of course I refused to sanction his insanity, and offered to establish him in business if he would behave himself sensibly."

"That is, if he would n't love anybody?"

"Precisely."

"And then what did *he* say?" asked Prudence, leaning on her guardian's arm persuasively, and smiling up in his face.

Mr. Dent was pleased to see that his ward took the matter with so much composure, and felt that the subject was one which could be treated best from a facetious point of view.

"He said he'd see me — no, he did not say that exactly; but he meant it. He declared he would go off somewhere and make his fortune in a few weeks, or hours, I forget which, and then come back and marry you — pretty much without consulting anybody's taste but his own. Upon my word, Prue, I think there is something wrong with his brain. He refused my advice and assistance point-blank."

"Then you quarrelled?"

"Yes, I suppose we quarrelled. He was as unreasonable as a lunatic. He cut off my head," said Mr. Dent grimly.

"Cut off — your head?"

"Substantially. He snipped off the top of a thistle with his walking-stick, and looked me straight in the eye, as much as to say, 'Consider your head off!'"

"Oh!" cried Prue faintly. "But how did it end?"

"It ended by my forbidding him to come to the house."

Prue's hand slipped from her guardian's shoulder with a movement like lightning.

"You turned him out of doors!"

"Well, perhaps that is stating it rather strongly."

"It was generous of him not to speak of his love to me, and brave of him to go to you — and you have turned him out of doors!" and Prue's eyes flashed curiously.

Now it was not, perhaps, a frightful thing in itself, Prue's eyes flashing; but since she was a baby, when her eyes could not flash, she had never given Mr. Dent such a look, and it all but withered him. It was so sudden and unlike her!

"Why, Prue!" he managed to cry, "you don't mean to say you love the fellow!"

"But how did it end?"

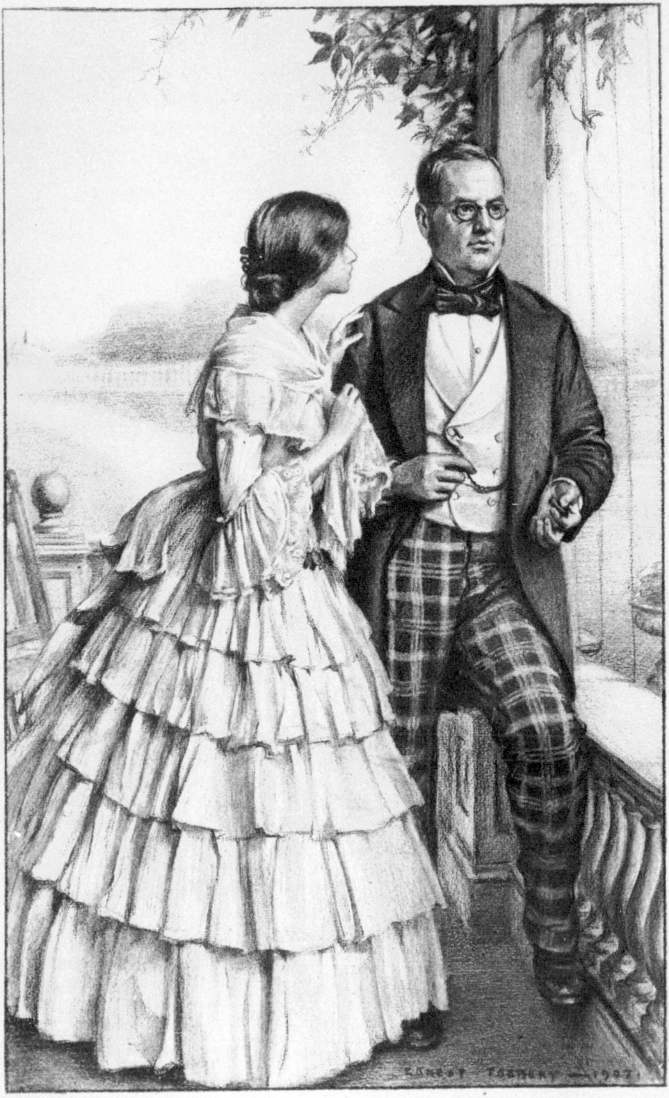

"I do love him!" cried Prudence, with red cheeks. "I did n't love him, but you have made me love him! I have beggared him, and made him wretched besides, and I 'd marry him to-morrow if he 'd ask me!"

"Gracious heaven, Prue! what else could I do?"

"You ought to have sent him to *me!*"

Struck by this reply into "amazement and admiration," Mr. Dent found no words at his command as the girl glided by him and into the house.

"And Prue loves him," he said in a subdued voice, leaning against the balustrade heavily, like a wounded man, "my Prue!"

Between his nephew and his ward Mr. Ralph Dent had had a hard day of it.

If John Dent could have caught only an echo of Prudence Palfrey's words as she swept by her guardian that afternoon, he would not have been the forlorn creature he was, over there in Rivermouth, trying to read musty books on knotty doctrinal points, borrowed from Parson Hawkins's library, but forever leaving them to wander down to points on the river, where was afforded what the poet Gray would have called "a distant prospect" of Willowbrook chimneys.

A week had passed since the rupture with his uncle, and Dent's plans were matured. He had fallen in with a brother knight-errant, a Rivermouth boy and quondam schoolmate of his, and the two had agreed to set forth together in search of fortune. Their plan was to go to San Francisco overland, and, failing of adventures there, to push on to the mining districts. It was a mad idea, and John Dent's own. The day had long gone by when great nuggets were unearthed by private enterprise in California; but he had drawn the notion into his brain that his fortune was to be made at the mines. How or when the fancy first took possession of him I cannot say. Perhaps the accounts of the Australian gold-fields, then a comparatively recent discovery, had something to do with it; perhaps it was born solely of his necessity. He wanted money, he wanted a large quantity, and he wanted it immediately. A gold-mine seemed to simplify the matter. To bring it down to a fine point, it was a gold-mine he wanted. He brooded over the subject until it became a fixed fact in his mind that there was a huge yellow nugget waiting for him somewhere, hidden in the emerald side of a mountain or lying in the bed of some pebbly stream among the gulches. Æons and æons ago Nature had secreted it in her bounteous bosom to lavish it lovingly on some man adventurous and faithful above the rest. The Golden Fleece at Colchis was not more real to Jason and his crew than this nugget finally became to John Dent. He was a poet in those days. Every man is a poet at some period of his life, if only for half an hour.

In Parson Hawkins's library was a work on metallography, together with a certain history of the gold-fever in the early days of California: young Dent had pored over these volumes as Cervantes' hero pored over the books on chivalry, until his brain was a little touched; and also like the simple gentleman of La Mancha, John Dent had not been long in finding a simpler soul to inoculate with his madness — to wit, Deacon Twombly's son Joe.

Their preparations for the journey were completed, and Joseph Twombly, set on fire by his comrade's enthusiasm, was burning to be gone; but John Dent lingered irresolutely day after day in the old town by the river. An unconquerable longing had grown up in his heart to say good-by to Prudence Palfrey.

In the meanwhile the days were passing tranquilly but not happily at Willowbrook.

Mr. Dent was silent and gloomy, and Prudence had lost her high spirits. She had also lost a rose or two from her cheek, but they came back impetuously whenever she thought of the confession she had made to her guardian. It had been almost as much a surprise to herself as to him. John Dent's name had not been breathed by either since that afternoon. Whether he was still at Rivermouth or not, neither knew. Both had cast a hasty glance over the congregation, on entering the church the succeeding Sunday, one half dreading and the other half hoping he might be there; but John Dent, seated in the gallery behind the choir, had eluded them. He sat with his eyes riveted on the back of Prue's best bonnet, and it had not done the young man any appreciable good.

As matters stood Prudence could not, and Mr. Dent did not, go to Rivermouth. Having declared to him that she loved a man who had not asked her for her love, she had cut herself off from the town while young Dent remained there. This involved a serious deprivation to Prue, for she longed to carry her trouble to the good old parson in Horseshoe Lane, who had been her counsellor and comforter in all her tribulations as far back as she could remember.

Towards the end of the second week Prudence became restless. No doubt John Dent had quitted the place long ago. And suppose he had not? suppose he had decided to live there? Was she to shut herself up forever like a nun? There were calls owing in town, at the Blydenburghs' and elsewhere. The whole routine and pleasure of life was not to be interrupted because her uncle had quarrelled with his nephew.

At the breakfast-table she said, "I am going to town this morning, uncle."

"Will you have the phaeton?" asked Mr. Dent, but not with effusion, as the French say.

"I think I shall walk, for the sake of the exercise."

"But, Prue" —

"If you infer that I am going to town to hunt up a young man who ran away from me," Prudence broke out with a singular dash of impatience, "I will stay at home."

"I do not infer anything of the kind," Mr. Dent answered. "I was simply going to say you had better ride; it is dusty walking."

Prudence bit her lip.

"I want you to be your own sensible self, Prue. You are very strange recently. Many a time you must have felt the lack of a gentler hand than mine to guide you. You never needed guidance more than now. I wish I knew what wise words Mercy would speak to her child, if she were alive."

Prudence rose from her chair and went over to his side.

"If my mother were here, I think she would tell me to ask your forgiveness for all the annoyance I have been to you from the time I was a baby until now. I am very sorry for the way I spoke the other day. I could not help l-liking John Dent, but I needn't have been a fierce wolf about it, need I?"

Mr. Dent smiled at the fierce wolf, but he could not help recognizing the appositeness of simile. It was the first time he had smiled in two weeks, and it was to Prudence like a gleam of pure sunshine after dog-days. So the cloud between them broke, floated off a little way, and halted; for life to these two was never to be just what it had been.

"If you don't wish me to go" — said Prue meekly.

"But I do," Mr. Dent answered. Then he made a forlorn effort to be merry, and bade her hurry off to town and get married, and come back again as soon as possible.

And Prue said she would. She resolved, however, that if by any chance John Dent was still in Rivermouth, and if by any greater chance she encountered him — and nothing was more remote from her design — she would behave with faultless discretion. She would not marry him to-morrow, now, if he asked her; she loved him, but her love should never be a millstone about his neck. That phrase of her guardian's had sunk into her mind.

As she drew near the town, and saw the roof-tops and spires taking sharper outlines against the delicate lilac sky, her pulse quickened. What if she were to meet him on the bridge, or run against him suddenly at a street corner? Would his conceit lead him to suppose she was searching for him, or even wished to meet him?

The thought sent the blood blooming up to her temples, and she was half inclined to turn back. Then, with a little imperious toss of the head, like a spirited pony taking the bit between its teeth, she went on.

Prudence avoided the main thoroughfares, and, by a circuitous route through Pickering's Court, reached the gate of the parsonage without accident. She closed the gate behind her carefully, with a dim apprehension that if she let it swing to with a bang, John Dent, walking somewhere a mile or two away, might hear the click of the latch and be down on her. An urchin passing the house at that instant gave a shrill whistle through his fingers, in facile imitation of a steam-engine, and the strength went quite out of Prue's knees. Smiling at her own nervousness she ran up the gravelled walk.

At the farther end of the piazza, completely screened by vines from the street, sat John Dent, with corrugated brow, reading Adam Smith on The Wealth of Nations.

As Prudence stretched out her hand towards the knocker, the young man looked up wearily from the book and saw her, and then her eyes fell upon him.

"I — I thought you had gone!" stammered Prudence, grasping at the flat-nosed brass cherub for support.

"No, I have n't gone yet," replied John Dent, with beaming countenance.

"So I see," said Prue, recovering herself.

"I hated to go without saying good-by to you, and of course I could not come to the house."

"Of course not," said Prue.

"And so I waited."

"Waited for me to come to you!" cried Prue, flushing. "You might have waited a long time if I had suspected it."

"And you would n't have come?"

"No."

A No kept on ice for a twelvemonth could not have been colder than that.

"Are you angry with me, too?"

"I am very angry with you. You were entirely in the wrong to quarrel with your uncle, John Dent; he was your only friend."

"He left me no choice, you see. I went to him in great trouble and uncertainty, wanting kindly advice, and he treated me harshly, as I think. Unless he has told you why we fell out, I shall say nothing about it. Did he tell you, Prue?"

"Yes, he told me," said Prudence slowly.

"What could I do but go to him?"

"I was very sorry it happened."

"What if I had come to you instead?"

"I should have been still more sorry."

"Then after all," said John Dent, "it seems that I chose the lesser evil. There is some small merit in that. But the mischief is done — the cat has eaten the canary — and the only atonement I can make is to take myself off as soon as may be. I cannot tell you what a comfort it is to see you once more. I have spent two or three hours here every day, hoping some lucky chance would bring you. Parson Wibird, you know, was my father's most intimate friend when our family lived in the town, and I did n't seem to have any one nearer to me; so I 've given him a good deal of my unpleasant society. I have been reading the parson's theological works," he went on, with a dreary air, "and some books on mining, and I'm pretty well up on the future state and geology."

It was all Prudence could do not to laugh.

"But the minutes hung on my hands, I can tell you. About the wretchedest hours of my life I have passed on that little pine seat yonder."

Many a time afterwards Prudence recalled these words, sitting disconsolately herself on that same green bench under the vines.

"All that is past, now you are here; but I don't believe I could have stood it another week, even with the hope of seeing you at the end of it. Cousin Prue, there are several things I want to say to you; I hardly know how to say them. May I try?"

"That depends on what they are," returned Prudence. "There are some things which you should not say to me."

"I may tell you I love you?"

"No, you must not tell me that."

"I need not, you mean. Uncle Ralph has saved me the confusion of confession. If he had trusted me fully I believe I should have gone away with the word unspoken. I don't see the harm of speaking it now. I am very proud of loving you. I know I have laid up a store of unhappiness, may be one that will last me my days; but I shall never regret it. I stand higher in my own estimation that I could n't live in the same house with you week after week and not love you."

"But I — I never gave you" —

"Now you are on dangerous ground," said John Dent. "If you hate me, don't tell me; if you love me, don't tell me, for I could not bear that either. I pledge you my honor I don't know, I only hope, and would not know for the world."

Here was a lover — one man out of ten thousand — who was ready to bind himself hand and foot for his sweetheart, and would have no vows from her, even if she were willing to make them. He said nothing less than the truth when he declared his ignorance of the nature of Prue's feelings. She liked him, of course — that went without saying; but further than that he did not know. He was content to go away with so much hope as lies in uncertainty, and perhaps he was wise.

"You speak of love and hate," said Prudence, tracing a hieroglyphic on the piazza with the toe of her boot, "as if there was nothing between. What prevents me from being your friend? Your plans and welfare interest me very deeply, and I am glad of the chance to talk with you about them. Where are you going when you leave Rivermouth?"

"To California."

"So far!"

"I am going to the mines — the only short cut to fortune open to me. I'm sadly in lack of that kind of nerve which enables a man to plod on year in and year out for a mere subsistence. I am not afraid of hard work; I am ready to crowd the labor of half a lifetime into a few months for the sake of having the result in a lump. But I must have it in a lump. I won't accept fortune in driblets. I don't think I would stoop to pick up less than an ounce of gold at a time. I've a conviction, Prue, I shall light on some fat nuggets; they can't all have been found."

"I hope not," responded Prudence, smiling.

John Dent did not smile. As he spoke, his face flushed, and a lambent glow came into his eyes, as if he saw rich masses of the yellow ore cropping out among Parson Hawkins's marigold-beds.

"I have a theory," he said, "that a man never wants a thing as I want this, and is willing to pay the price for it, without getting it. I mean to come back independent, or not at all. I have discovered that a man without money in his pocket, or the knack to get it, had better be in his family tomb — if he has a family tomb. That is about the only place

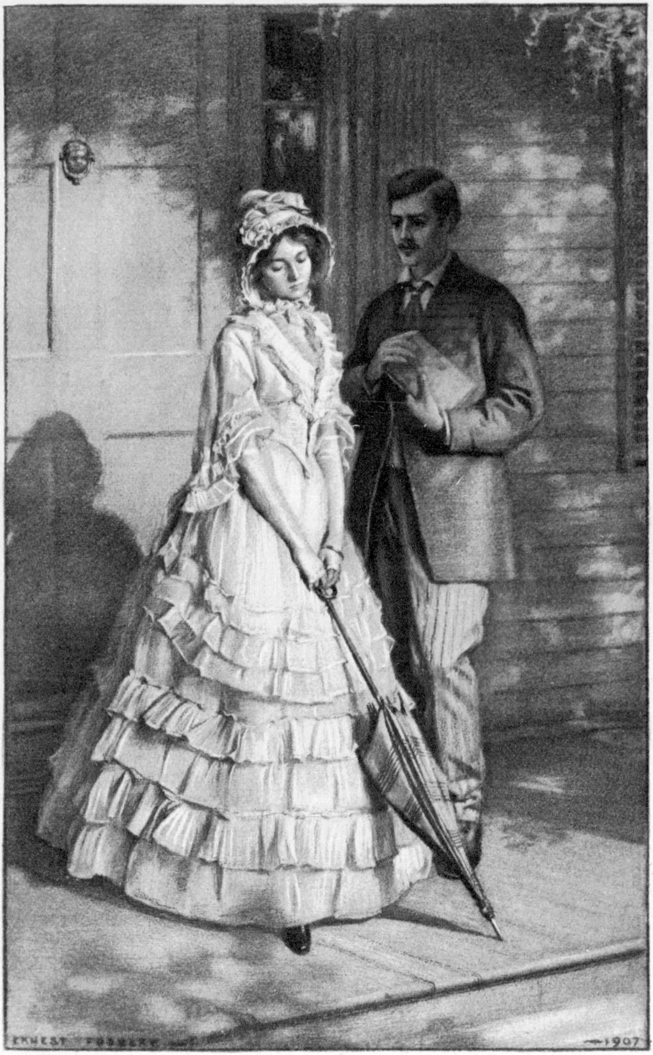
1907

where he will not be in the way. Moralists, surrounded by every luxury, frown down on what they call the lust of riches. It is one of the noblest of human instincts. The very pen and paper, and the small amount of culture which enables these ungrateful fellows to write their lopsided essays, would have been impossible without it. Some one has said this before — but not so well," added John Dent complacently, suddenly conscious that he was hammering away at one of Mr. Arthur Helps's ideas. "There was more sound sense in Iago's advice than he gets credit for. I mean to put money in my purse, Prue, and then come back to Rivermouth, and ask you to be my wife. There, I have said it. Are you angry?"

"N-o, not very," said Prudence, a little flurried. "But suppose I have married 'auld Robin Gray' in the meantime?" she added slyly.

"You are free to do it."

"And you'll not scowl at him, and make a scene of it when you come back?"

"I shall hate him," cried John Dent, as a venerable figure of a possible "auld Robin Gray" limped for an instant before his mind's eye. "No, Prue; I shall have no right to hate him. I shall only envy him. Perhaps I'll be magnanimous if he's a poor man —

though he was n't poor in the ballad — and turn over my wealth to him; it would be of no use to me without you. Then I'd go back to the wilds again."

He said this with a bleak laugh, and Prudence smiled, and her heart was as heavy as lead. It required an effort not to tell him that she would not marry though he stayed away a thousand years. If John Dent had asked Prudence that moment if she loved him, she would have thrown her cautious resolves to the winds; if he had asked her to go to the gold-fields with him, she would have tightened her bonnet-strings under her chin, and placed her hand in his. But the moment went by.

Prudence had moved away from the front door, and seated herself on the small bench at the end of the piazza, much to the chagrin of the Widow Mugridge, who had been feverishly watching the interview, and speculating on its probable nature, from a rear attic window across the street.

"I must go now," said Prudence, rising hastily. "I promised Uncle Ralph not to be long. I'm afraid I have been long. He will wonder what has kept me, and I have not seen the parson yet."

"I suppose I may write to you?" said John Dent. "I shall want to write only two letters," he added quickly; "one on my arrival at the mines, and one some months afterwards, to tell you the result of the expedition. As I shall send these letters under cover to Uncle Dent, there will be no offence. I do not ask you to answer them."

"He cannot object to that," said Prudence. "In spite of what has passed, I am sure he will be glad to hear of your movements, and anxious for your success."

"I am not so positive on that head."

"You do him injustice, then," returned Prudence warmly. "You don't know how good he is."

"I know how good he is n't."

"You mistake him entirely. He was willing to look upon you as his own son."

"But not as his son-in-law," suggested John Dent.

"He has not told me the particulars of the conversation," said Prudence, "but I am convinced he said nothing to you that was not wise and kind and candid."

"It was certainly candid."

"I see we shall not agree on this subject; let us speak of something pleasanter. When are you going away?"

"My going away is a pleasanter subject, then?"

"Yes, because it is something we cannot easily quarrel over."

"I shall leave Rivermouth to-morrow. Now that I have seen you, there is nothing to detain us."

"Us? you don't go alone, then?"

"No; Joe Twombly is going with me; you know him, the deacon's son. A very good fellow, Joe. His family made a great row at first. He had to talk over the two old folks, six grown sisters, the twins, and the baby. He's been bidding them good-by ever since the week before last. I quite envy him the widespread misery he is causing. I have only you and Parson Hawkins in the whole world to say good-by to, and you can't begin to be as sorry as six sisters."

"But I can be as sorry as one," said Prue, giving him her ungloved hand, and not withdrawing it. It was as white and cold as a snow-flake.

"I'd like to know what that Palfrey gal's a-doin' with Squire Dent's nevy on the parson's front piazza," muttered the Widow Mugridge, as she stretched her pelican-like neck out of the attic window.

"What, Prue! — you're not crying?"

"Yes, I am," said Prudence, looking up through two tears which had been troubling

PRUDENCE PALFREY

her some time. "Cannot a sister cry if she wants to?"

"If you are my sister" — And John Dent hesitated.

Prudence gave a little sob.

"If you are my sister, you will let me kiss you good-by."

"Yes," said Prudence.

Then John Dent stooped down and kissed her.

"Hoity-toity! what's this?" cried Parson Hawkins, appearing suddenly in the doorway with one finger shut in a vast folio, and his spectacles pushed up on his forehead, giving him the aspect of some benevolent four-eyed monster.

"There's the parson now," soliloquized the Widow Mugridge. "Mebbe he did n't come 'fore he's wanted. Sech goin's on!"

As Prue drew back, she pressed into John Dent's hand a little bunch of fuchsias which she had worn at her throat; he thanked her with a look, and was gone.

So the two parted — Prudence Palfrey to resume the quiet, colorless life of Willowbrook, and John Dent to go in search of his dragons.

VI

CONCERNING A SKELETON IN A CLOSET

Prue, on returning home, said nothing to her guardian touching the interview with John Dent at the parsonage.

She did not intend to hide the matter, but it was all too new and distracting for her to speak about just then. She was flurried, and wanted time to think it over. She lay awake half the night thinking of it, and began reproaching herself for her coldness and coquetry. How generous John Dent had been with her, and how calculating and worldly wise she had been on her part. He was going away to face hardship and danger, perhaps death itself, for her sake — she understood clearly it was for her sake — and she had let him go without speaking the word that would have made this comparatively easy for him. It was true, he had begged her not to speak the word; but she might have spoken it like an honest girl. She had given him a marble cheek to salute, when she ought to have thrown her arms around his neck. What was there to prevent her loving him and telling him so?

The generosity had been wholly on the side of her lover, and no woman is content with that; so Prue's heart warmed to him all the more because she had not been allowed to sacrifice herself in the least, and she fell asleep with the vow upon her lips that if she did not marry John Dent she would never marry.

At the breakfast-room door the next morning, Prudence met her guardian returning from a walk. He had been marketing at Rivermouth bright and early, and had had the unlooked-for satisfaction of beholding at a distance his nephew and Joseph Twombly standing in the midst of their luggage on the platform of the railroad station. But it chanced that on the way home Mr. Dent had picked up a piece of intelligence which turned the edge of his satisfaction.

"Laws a mercy, if that ain't Mr. Ralph Dent!" cried a shrill, querulous voice at his elbow, as that gentleman turned into Penhallow Place. It was the Widow Mugridge sweeping the flag-stones in front of her domicile. "Who'd 'a' thought you'd ketch me tidyin' up a bit this airly in the mornin'! It's the airly bird that gets the worm, Mr. Dent. Ben to see your nevy off to Californy, I s'pose! I see him an' Miss Prudence a-chirpin' thicker 'n blackbirds over there on the parson's piazzer yesterday forenoon, an' thought likely 's not he was goin' away at last. An' Joe, too — dear me! They do say Deacon Twombly's folks is dreffully cut up" —

Buz, buz, buz! Mr. Dent did not wait to hear more, but lifting his hat to the old lady, hurried down the street.

"I'd wager a cooky, now," said the good soul, leaning on the broom-handle meditatively, and following Mr. Dent's vanishing figure with a lack-lustre blue eye — "I'd wager a cooky, now, young Dent has ben settin' up to that Palfrey gal, an' there's ben trouble. Thought so all 'long. Clem Hoyt fetched away young Dent's trunk more 'n two weeks ago, and he hasn't set in the family pew sence. Guess things muster ben purty lively up to Willowbrook house. Well, now, it's cur'ous, how folks will fall to sixes an' sevins, 'specially relations, right in the face of their Creater!"

Mr. Dent gave Prudence a frigid good-morning. He had no heart to arraign her for her seeming duplicity; he had no heart for anything. Prue loved his nephew, and the two had met — met in secret. One had defied him and the other had deceived him.

I scarcely know how to describe the emotions

and perplexities that beset Mr. Dent at this period, without shearing him of some of those practical attributes which I have claimed for him.

When his nephew, that day on the road to Rivermouth, declared his intentions regarding Prue, Mr. Dent was startled and alarmed. That Prudence would marry some time or other, had occurred to him faintly as a possibility — a possibility so far in the future as not to be considered; but John Dent had taught him that the time was come when his hold on Prue would be slight, were the right man to demand her. John Dent was clearly not the right man, and Mr. Dent had opposed the arrangement, chiefly, as he imagined, because his nephew was not in a position to marry; but under it all was a strangely born and indefinable jealousy. Prue's declaration on the piazza that afternoon fell upon Mr. Dent like lightning from a cloudless sky; by the flash of her love he saw the depth of his own affection. It sometimes happens, outside the covers of romances, that a man rears an adopted girl from the cradle, and falls in love with her when she gets into long dresses — that the love creeps into existence unsuspected, and asserts itself suddenly, full-grown. It was something very like this that had happened to Mr. Dent.

There is said to be a skeleton in every house. Until then there had never been a skeleton at Willowbrook, at least since Mr. Dent owned the property; but there was one now, and Mr. Dent's task henceforth was to see that the ghastly thing did not peep out of its closet. Prudence should never dream of its existence; he would stand a grim sentinel over the secret until the earth covered him and it. He thought it hard, after the disappointment of his youth, that such a burden should be laid upon his later years; but he would bear it as he had borne the other.

He saw his duty plainly enough, but there were almost insuperable difficulties in the performance of it. It was next to impossible for him to meet Prudence on the same familiar footing as formerly; the unrestrained intimacy that had held between them was full of peril for his secret. He must be always on his guard lest she should catch a glimpse of the Bluebeard chamber where he had hidden his stifled love. An unconsidered word or look might be a key to it. Now it so fell out, in his perplexity as to which was the least dangerous method to pursue, that this amiable and honest gentleman began treating the girl with a coldness and constraint which gradually merged into a degree of harshness he was far from suspecting.

Acknowledging to herself that she had given her guardian some grounds for displeasure, Prudence was ready to make any advances towards a reconciliation; but Mr. Dent gave her no encouragement; he was ice to her. At this stage business called him to Boston, where he remained a fortnight.

"He will forgive me before he comes home," Prudence said to herself; but he came home as he went away, gelid.

As she leaned over his chair at bedtime that night to offer him her forehead to kiss, a pretty fashion which had outlived her childhood, he all but repulsed her. Prue shrank back, and never attempted to repeat the caress.

"He is still angry," she thought, "because he fancies there is some engagement between me and John Dent."

But she was too proud now, as she had been too timid before, to tell him what had passed at Parson Hawkins's. He evidently knew they had met there; she had forfeited his confidence and respect, and that was hard to bear, harder than John Dent's absence, a great deal. She would have borne that cheerfully if her guardian had let her; but he made even that heavier.

The old parson was Prue's only resource at

this time. Whenever household duties gave her leave, she went straight to the parsonage, and sat for hours on the little green bench under the vines, nearly leafless now, where John Dent had waited for her. She called it her stool of penitence. Here she actually read through Adam Smith on The Wealth of Nations, a feat which I venture to assert has been accomplished by few young women in New England or elsewhere. It was like a novel to her.

Sometimes the parson would bring his armchair out on the piazza into the sunshine, and the two would hold long discourses on California and John Dent; for the parson had a fondness for the young fellow; he had taught Jack Latin when he was a kid; besides, the boy's father had been dear to him. How far the young man had taken Parson Hawkins into his confidence, I do not know; but it is presumable that Prudence told her old friend all there was to tell. Often the parson was absent from home, visiting parishioners, and Prudence sat there alone, thinking of John Dent. She had fallen into so pitiable a state that this became her sole pleasure — to walk a mile and a quarter to a place where she could be thoroughly miserable.

These frequent pilgrimages to Horseshoe

Lane filled Mr. Dent with lively jealousy. He grew to hate the simple old gentleman, whose society was openly preferred to his own, though he did not make his own too agreeable.

He blamed the parson for coming between him and Prudence; most of all he blamed him for allowing John Dent to meet her clandestinely under his roof. He made no doubt but the intriguing old woman — for what was he but an old woman? — had connived at the meeting, very likely brought it about. Perhaps he saw a pitiful marriage-fee at the end of his plots and his traps, the wretched old miser!

If Prudence was rendered unhappy by her guardian's harsh humor, he was touched to the heart by her apparent indifference. They saw each other rarely now, only at meals and sometimes in the sitting-room after dinner. Mr. Dent spent his time mostly in the library, and Prudence kept out of the way. She no longer played chess with him or read to him of an evening. The autumn evenings were dull and interminable at Willowbrook. If it had been Mr. Dent's purpose to make Prudence miss his nephew every hour of the day, Machiavelli himself could not have improved on the course he was pursuing.

One afternoon, after nearly three months of this, Mr. Dent received an envelope from his nephew enclosing a letter for Prudence. Mr. Dent's first impulse was to throw the missive into the grate; but he followed his second impulse, and carried it to her, though it burnt his fingers like a hot coal.

Prudence started and colored when her eyes fell upon the superscription, but she made no motion to take the letter; she let it lie on the table where he had placed it.

"She wishes to read it alone," said Mr. Dent to himself bitterly. He was marching off to the door as stiff as a grenadier when Prudence intercepted him.

"Are we never going to be friends again?" she said, laying her hand lightly on his arm. "Are you never going to like me any more? I begin to feel that I am a stranger in the house; it is no longer my home as it was. Do you know what I shall do when I am convinced you have entirely ceased to care for me? I shall go away from you."

He gave a quick glance at Prudence's face, and saw that she meant it.

"Go away from me!" he exclaimed. "What in God's world could I do without you!"

"I cannot go on living here if you don't love me. I have done nothing to deserve your unkindness. I saw John Dent only by chance, I did not go to meet him, there is no engagement between us; but I love him, and shall love him always. I regret every day of my life that I did not tell him so, like an honest girl. That is really my only fault. For all this I ask your forgiveness so far as you consider yourself disobeyed. You have been unjustly severe with me. In a little while your severity will lose the power of wounding, and I shall think only of your injustice."

Then Prudence walked away and sat down by the work-table.

Every word of this was a dagger to Mr. Dent. Had he been cruel to her? It was plain he had. He was struck now by the change that had taken place in Prudence within three months. He had not noticed until then how pale she was; there were dark circles under her eyes that seemed to darken her whole face, and the eyes themselves were grown large and lustrous, like a consumptive's. As her hands lay in her lap, he observed how white and thin they were; and his conscience smote him. It was not enough he should keep the skeleton securely locked in its closet; his duty went further; the girl's health and happiness were to be looked after a little, and he had neglected that.

"Prue," he said, with sudden remorse, "I have been very blind and unreasonable. Only be a happy girl again, and I will ask you to do nothing else except to forgive me for not finding it easy to yield you up to the first young fellow that came along and asked for you. You have been my own girl for so many years, that the thought of losing you distracted me. But we won't speak about that. Write to Jack, and tell him to come home; he shall be welcome to Willowbrook. I 'll bury a bushel of gold eagles in the lawn for him to dig up, if he is still mad on the subject. All I have is yours and his. What do I care for beyond your happiness?" And Mr. Dent put his arm around Prudence and kissed her much the same as he might have done before John Dent ever came to Rivermouth.

The wisest way to treat a skeleton is to ignore it. There is nothing a skeleton likes more than coddling: nothing it likes less than neglect. Neglect causes it to pine away — if a skeleton, even in a metaphor, can be said to pine away — and crumble into dust.

"And now," cried Mr. Dent, "let us see what the young man has to say for himself."

He never did things by halves, this honest gentleman. When he made beer he made the best beer Rivermouth ever tasted; though he was no longer proud of it.

He picked up the letter and handed it to

Prudence, who could not speak for surprise and joy over this sudden transformation. She sat motionless for a minute, with her eyes bright with tears, and then broke the seal.

"I'll read it aloud," said Prue primly, as one with authority.

The letter was not from California, as they had expected, but was dated at an obscure little post-village with a savage name somewhere on the frontiers of Montana.

Bewildering rumors of gold discoveries in the Indian Territory had caused a change in the plans of the adventurers at the last moment.[1] Instead of proceeding to San Francisco, they had struck for the other side of the Rocky Mountains. They were now on their way to the new gold regions. At Salt Lake City, where they had halted to purchase mining implements, tents, provisions, etc., John Dent had been too busy to write; he did not know when he would be able to write again; probably not for several months. They were going into the wilds where postal arrangements were of the most primitive order. The country was said to be infested by bushwhackers, on the lookout for unprotected baggage-trains bound for the diggings, and for lucky

[1] In point of fact, the discovery of gold in Montana took place at a period somewhat later than that indicated here.

miners returning with their spoils. Besides, scouting parties of the Bannock tribe had an ugly fashion of waylaying the mail and decorating their persons with cancelled postage-stamps. Under these circumstances communication with the States would be difficult and might be impossible. Dent and Twombly were travelling with a body of forty or fifty men, among whom certain claims already secured were to be divided on their arrival at the point of destination in Red Rock Cañon. Their special mess consisted of Twombly, Dent, and a young man named Nevins, whom they had picked up at Salt Lake City. This Nevins, it appeared, had made a fortune in California in '56, and lost it in some crazy silver-mining speculation two years before. He had come over with a crowd from Nevada, and found himself in Salt Lake City with one suit of clothes and a large surplus of unemployed pluck. He was thoroughly up in gold-digging, a very superior fellow in every way, and would be of immense service to the tyros. The three were to work on shares, Nevins putting his knowledge and experience against their capital and ignorance. John Dent was in high spirits.

If there was any gold in Montana, he and Twombly and Nevins had sworn to have it.

PRUDENCE PALFREY

There was no doubt of the gold; and three bold hearts and three pairs of strong hands were going to seek it all they knew. "I thank my stars," he wrote, "that Uncle Dent opposed me as he did in a certain matter; if he had not, I should probably at this moment be lying around New York on a beggarly salary, instead of marching along with a score or so of brave fellows to pick up a princely fortune in Red Rock Cañon."

"Well, I hope he will pick up the princely fortune, with all my heart," remarked Mr. Dent, when they came to the end of the disjointed and incoherent four pages.

There was not a word of love in them, and no allusion to the past, except the passage quoted, and the reading had been without awkwardness.

Prue was relieved, for she had broken the seal with some doubt as to the effect of a love-letter on her guardian even in his present blissful mood; and Mr. Dent himself was well satisfied with the absence of sentiment, though the spirit underlying the letter was evident enough.

"If I were a man," Prudence said, "I would not be a clerk in a shop, or sit all day like a manikin on a stool with a pen stuck behind my ear, while new worlds full of riches and adventures lay wide open for gallant souls. Cousin John was right to go, and I would not have him return, until he has done his best like a man. It will be a great thing for him, uncle, it will teach him self-assurance and " —

"But, Prue, dear, I don't think that was a quality he lacked," put in Mr. Dent, with a twinkle in his eye.

"Well, it will do him good, anyhow," said Prue didactically; then, sinking her voice to a minor key and sweeping her guardian from head to foot with her silken lashes, she added, "and I do not mind so much his being away, now you are kind to me. What trouble could be unbearable while I can turn to you who have been father, mother, lover, and all the world to me!"

She was rewarding him for his concessions. The words dropped like honey from the girl's lips. An hour before they would have been full of bitterness to him; but he was a new man within these sixty minutes; he had trampled his folly under foot, and was ready to accept as very precious the only kind of affection she had to give him. The color must be lured back into those cheeks and the troubled face taught to wear its happy look again. What a cruel egotist he had been, nursing his own preposterous fancies and breaking down the health of the girl!

"A perfect dog in the manger," he said to himself, as he marched up and down the garden walks, in the afternoon sunshine, with a lighter heart than he had carried for many a week. "And what a sentimental old dog! I shall be writing verses next, and printing them in the poet's corner in the Rivermouth Barnacle. I declare I am alarmed about myself. A man ought n't to be in his dotage at fifty-six. If Jack knew of this he would be justified in placing me in the State Lunatic Asylum."

So Mr. Dent derided himself pleasantly that afternoon, and said severer things of his conduct than I am disposed to set down here, though it is certainly a great piece of folly for a young lad of fifty-six to fall in love with an old lady of eighteen — particularly when she is his ward, and especially when she loves his nephew.

The four or five months that succeeded the receipt of John Dent's letter sped swiftly and happily over the Willowbrook people. Mr. Dent was, if anything, kinder to Prudence than he had ever been. His self-conquest was so complete that on several occasions he led himself in chains, so to speak, to the parsonage, and took a morbid pleasure in playing backgammon with the old clergyman.

No further tidings had come to them from John Dent; but Prudence had been prepared for a long silence, and did not permit this to disturb her. She was her own self again, filling the house with sunshine.

Mr. Dent said to her one day: "Prue, I really believe that you love Jack."

Prudence beamed upon him.

"What made you?" asked her guardian thoughtfully.

"He did."

"I suppose so; but I don't see how he did it."

"Well, then, you did."

"I?"

"Yes — by opposing us!"

"Oh, if I had shut my eyes and allowed Jack to make love to you, then you would n't have loved him?"

"Possibly not."

"I wish I had let him!"

"I wish you had," said Prue demurely.

"It was obstinacy, then?"

"Just sheer obstinacy," said Prue, turning a hem and smoothing it on her knee with the rosy nail of her forefinger. Then she leaned one elbow on the work, and, resting her chin on her palm, looked up into her guardian's face after the manner of that little left-hand cherub in the foreground of Raphael's Madonna di San Sisto.

Mr. Dent went on with his newspaper, leaving Prue in a brown study.

The period preceding John Dent's visit seemed to Prudence like some far-off historical epoch with which she could not imagine herself contemporary. Her existence had been so colorless before, made up of unimportant happy nothings. It was so full now of complicated possibilities. A new future had opened upon her, all unlike that eventless one she had been in the habit of contemplating, in which she was to glide from merry girlhood with its round hats, into full-blown spinstership with its sedate bonnets, and thence into serene old age with its prim caps and silver-bowed spectacles — mistress of Willowbrook in these various stages, placidly pouring out tea for her guardian and executing *chefs-d'œuvre* in worsted to be sold for the benefit of the heathen.

This tranquil picture — with that vague background of cemetery which *will* come into pictures of the future — had not been without its charm for Prudence. To grow old leisurely in that pleasant old mansion among the willows, and to fall asleep in the summer or winter twilight after an untroubled, secluded-violet sort of life, had not appeared so hard a fate to her.

But now it seemed to Prudence that that would be a very hard fate indeed.

In the meanwhile the days wore on, not unhappily, as I have said. Nearly a year went by, and then Prudence began to share the anxiety of the Twombly family, who had heard nothing from Joseph since the enclosure sent in John Dent's letter.

"You remember what he wrote about the uncertainty of the mails," said Mr. Dent cheeringly. "More than likely the Bannock braves are at this moment seated around the council-fire, with all their war-paint on, perusing Jack's last epistle, and wondering what the deuce he is driving at."

Prue laughed, but her anxiety was not dispelled by the suggestion. She had a presentiment which she could not throw off that all was not well with the adventurers. What might not happen to them, among the desperate white men and lawless savages, out there in the Territory? Mr. Dent called her his little pocket Cassandra, and tried to laugh down her fancies; but in the midst of his pleasantries and her forebodings a letter came — a letter which Prudence read with blanched lip and cheek, and then laid away, to grow yellow with time, in a disused drawer of the old brass-mounted writing-desk that stood in her bedroom. It was a letter with treachery and shipwreck and despair in it. A great calamity had befallen John Dent. He had made his pile — and lost it. But how he made it and how he lost it must be told by itself.

VII

HOW JOHN DENT MADE HIS PILE AND LOST IT

It is an epic that ought to be sung at length, if one had the skill and the time; but I have neither the time nor the skill, and must make a ballad of it. The material of this chapter is drawn chiefly from Joseph Twombly's verbal narrative, and the fragments of a journal which John Dent kept at intervals in those days.

It was an afternoon in the latter part of September that the party with which Dent and Twombly and Nevins had associated themselves drew rein, on a narrow bridle-path far up the side of a mountain in eastern Montana. Rising in their stirrups, and holding on by the pommels of their saddles, they leaned over the sheer edge of the precipice and saw the Promised Land lying at their feet. On one side of an impetuous stream, that ran golden in the reflected glow of the remoter peaks, lay a city of tents, pine-huts, and rude brush wakiups, from which spiral columns of smoke slowly ascended here and there, and melted as they touched the upper currents of the wind. Along the cañon, following the course of the stream, were hundreds of blue and red and gray figures moving about restlessly like ants. These were miners at work. Now and then the waning sunlight caught the point of an uplifted pick, and it sparkled like a flake of mica.

It was a lonely spot. All this busy human life did not frighten away the spirit of isolation that had brooded over it since the world was made. Shut in by savage hills, stretching themselves cloudward like impregnable battlements, it seemed as if nothing but a miracle had led the foot of man to its interior solitude. What a lovely, happy nook it seemed, flooded with the ruddy stream of sunset! No wonder the tired riders halted on the mountain-side, gazing down half doubtingly upon its beauty.

"Dent," whispered George Nevins impressively, "there is gold here." Then he sat motionless for a few minutes, taking in every aspect of the cañon. "What gold there is over yonder," he presently added, in the same low voice, "is pulverized, lying in secret crevices, or packed away in the sands of the river-bed; troublesome hard work to get it, too. How neatly Nature stows it away, confound her!"

"But there *is* gold?"

"Tons — for the man that can find the rich spots."

"And nuggets?"

"*And* nuggets."

"Let us go!" cried John Dent, plunging the spurs into his horse. The rest of the party, refreshed by the halt, followed suit, and the train swept down the mountain-path, the rowels and bells of their Spanish spurs jingling like mad.

So they entered the Montana diggings.

More than once on their journey to Red Rock, which had not been without its perils, Dent and Twombly had found Nevins's experience and readiness of great advantage to them, and that afternoon, on arriving at the cañon, they had fresh cause to congratulate themselves on having him for a comrade. Two diggers, who were working a pit below them on the ravine, had encroached on their claim, and seemed indisposed to relinquish a certain strip of soil next the stream very convenient for washing purposes. Nevins measured the ground carefully, coolly pulled up the stakes which had been removed, and set them back in their original holes. He smiled while he was doing this, but it was a wicked sort of smile, as dangerous as a sunstroke.

PRUDENCE PALFREY

The men eyed him sullenly for a dozen or twenty seconds; then one of them walked up to his mate and whispered in his ear, and then the pair strolled off, glancing warily from time to time over their shoulders.

Dent and Twombly looked on curiously. Dent would have argued the case, and proved to them, by algebra, that they were wrong; Twombly would have compromised by a division of the disputed tract; but Nevins was an old hand, and knew how to hold his own.

"The man who hesitates in this community is lost," said Nevins, turning to his companions. "If I had not meant fight, they would have shot me. As it was — I should have shot them."

"Why, Nevins!" cried Twombly, "what a bloodthirsty fellow you are, to be sure!"

"You wait," Nevins said. "You don't know what kind of crowd you have got into. Here and there, may be, there's an honest fellow, but as for the rest — jail-birds from the States, gamblers from San Francisco, roughs from Colorado and Nevada, and blackguards from everywhere. Our fellow-citizens in the flourishing town of Red Rock are the choice scum and sediment of society, and I shall be out of my reckoning if the crack of the revolver does n't become as familiar to our ears as the croak of the bullfrogs over there in the alders."

Nevins had not drawn a flattering picture of the inhabitants of Red Rock; but it was as literal as a photograph.

The rumors of a discovery of rich placer diggings in Montana had flown like wildfire through the Territories and the border States, and caused a stampede among the classes first affected by that kind of intelligence. Two months before, the valley was a solitude. Only the songs of birds, the plunge of a red-deer among the thickets, or the cry of some savage animal, broke its stillness. One day a trapper wandered by chance into the cañon, and got benighted there. In the morning, eating his breakfast, he had stuck his sheath-knife for convenience into the earth beside him; on withdrawing it he saw a yellow speck shining in the bit of dirt adhering to the blade. The trapper quietly got up and marked out his claim. He knew it could not be kept secret. A man may commit murder and escape suspicion, though "murder speaks with most miraculous organ;" but he may never hope to discover gold and not be found out.

Two months later there was a humming town in Red Rock Cañon, with a population of two thousand and upwards.

There was probably never a mining town of the same size that contained more desperadoes than Red Rock in the first year of its existence. Hither flocked all the ruffians that had made other localities too hot to hold them — gentlemen with too much reputation, and ladies with too little; and here was formed the nucleus of that gang of marauders, known as Henry Plummer's Road Agent Band, which haunted the mountain-passes, pillaging and murdering, until the Vigilantes took them in hand and hanged them with as short shrift and as scant mercy as they had given their fellow-men. That is a black page in the history of American gold-seeking which closes with the execution of Joe Pizanthia, Buck Stinson, Haze Lyons, Boone Helme, Erastus Yager, Dutch John, Club-foot George, and Bill Graves — their very names are a kind of murder.[1] And these were prominent citizens of Red Rock when our little party of adventurers set up their tent and went to work on their claim in the golden valley.

"Nevins has not mistaken the geological any more than he has the moral character of the

---

[1] An account of the careers of these men is to be found in a curious little work by Professor Thomas J. Dimsdale, of Virginia City, who narrowly escaped writing a very notable book when he wrote The Vigilantes of Montana.

cañon," writes John Dent in his journal under date of October 12. "Gold-dust has been found scattered all along the bed of the river, and in some instances lucky prospectors have struck rich pockets; but of those massive nuggets which used to drive men wild in the *annus mirabilis* '49 we have seen none yet, though there is a story afloat about a half-breed finding one as big as a cocoanut! I am modest myself, and am willing to put up with a dozen or twenty nuggets of half that size. It does n't become a Christian to be grasping. *Mem.* Digging for gold, however it may dilate the imagination in theory, is practically devilish hard work."

This is a discovery which it appears was made by our friends long before they discovered the gold itself. For a fortnight they toiled like Trojans; they gave themselves hardly time to eat; at night they dropped asleep like beasts of burden; and at the end of fourteen days they had found no gold. At the end of the third week they had made nearly a dollar a day each — half the wages of a day-laborer at the East. John Dent, with a heavy sigh, suggested that they had better look up a claim for a cemetery.

"I never like to win the first hand," said Nevins genially; "it brings bad luck."

"The fellows from Sacramento, down the stream, are taking out seven hundred a week," remarked Twombly.

"Our turn will come," Nevins replied, cheerly still, like Abou Ben Adhem to the Angel.

This was on Sunday. The trio had knocked off work, and so had the camp generally. Sunday was a gala day. The bar-rooms and the gambling-saloons were thronged; at sundown the dance-house would open — the Hurdy-Gurdy House, as it was called. Lounging about camp, but as a usual thing in close propinquity to some bar, were knots of unsuccessful diggers, anathematizing their luck and on the alert for an invitation to drink. All day Sunday an odor of mixed drinks floated up from Red Rock and hung over it in impalpable clouds.

The three friends strolled through the town on a tour of observation, and brought up at the door of a saloon where a crowd was gathered. A man had been shot at one of the tables, and his comrades were fetching him out, dead, with his derringer, still smoking, clutched in his hand. Following the corpse was a lame individual, apparently the chief mourner, carrying the dead man's hat on a stick. The crowd opened right and left to let the procession pass, and our friends came full upon it.

Dent and Twombly turned away, sickened by the spectacle. Nevins looked on with an expression of half-stimulated curiosity, and stroked his long, yellow beard.

"And this is Sunday," thought John Dent. "In Rivermouth, the old sexton is tolling the bell for the afternoon service ; Uncle Dent and my little girl are sitting in the high-backed wall-pew — I can see them now ! Uncle Dent preparing to go to sleep, Prue looking like a rose, and Parson Wibird, God bless his old white head ! going up the pulpit stairs in his best coat shiny at the seams. Outside are the great silver poplars, and the quiet street, and the sunshine like a blessing falling over all !"

The close atmosphere of the camp stifled him as he conjured up this picture. He longed to be alone, and, dropping silently behind his companions, wandered off beyond the last row of wakiups and out into the deserted ravine.

There he sat down under a ledge, and with his elbows resting on his knees, dreamed of the pleasant town by the sea, of Prudence and his uncle, and the old minister in Horseshoe Lane. Presently he took from his pocket-book a knot of withered flowers and leaves ; these he spread in the palm of his hand with great care, and held for half an hour or more, looking at them from time to time in a way that seemed idiotic to a solitary gentleman in a slouched hat and blanket-overcoat who was digging in a pit across the gully. What slight things will sometimes entertain a man when he is alone! This handful of faded fuchsia blossoms made John Dent forget the hundreds of weary miles that stretched between him and New England; holding it so, in his palm, it bore him through the air back to the little Yankee seaport as if it had been Fortunatus's magic cap.

It was sunset when Dent sauntered pensively into camp, meeting Twombly and Nevins on the outskirts, looking for him.

"Jack!" cried Twombly, "you have given me such a turn! It really is n't safe in this place for a fellow to go off mooning by himself. What on earth have you been doing?"

"Something quite unusual, Joseph — I've been thinking."

"Homesick, eh?" said Nevins.

"Just a little."

Then they walked on in silence. Nevins stopped abruptly.

"What is that?"

"A bit of rock I picked up out yonder; say what it is yourself." And Dent tossed the fragment to Nevins, who caught it deftly.

"Pyrites," said Nevins, flinging it away contemptuously. "Come and have some supper."

The instant they were inside the tent Nevins laid his hand on Dent's shoulder.

"Do you happen to remember the spot where you picked up that — bit of rock?"

"Yes, why?"

"Nothing — only it was as fine a specimen of silver as we shall be likely to see."

"Silver!" shouted John Dent, "and you threw it away!"

"I'll go get it directly, if you'll be quiet. Did you see those two fellows watching us? It behooves a man here to keep his eye open on the Sabbath day."

He was a character, this Nevins, in his way, though it would be difficult perhaps to state what his special way was. In the gulches, with pick and spade, he was simply a miner who knew his business thoroughly; on horseback he became a part of the horse like a Comanche; when a question in science or literature came up, as sometimes happened between him and Dent, he talked like a man who had read and thought. "Nevins has apparently received a collegiate education," John Dent writes in the diary, "and is certainly a gentleman, though what it is that constitutes a gentleman is an open question. It is not culture, for I have known ignorant men who were gentlemen, and learned scholars who were not; it is not money, nor grace, nor goodness, nor station. It is something indefinable, like poetry, and Nevins has it."

From the hour they met him at Salt Lake City, he had been a puzzle to the two New Englanders; his talents and bearing were so out of keeping with his circumstances. But, as for that matter, so were John Dent's. Nevins was candor itself, and if he said little of his past life, he did not hesitate to speak of it, and seemed to have nothing to conceal. One fact was clear to both our Rivermouth friends — Nevins was worth his weight in gold to them.

The piece of rock that John Dent had picked up on the mountain-side was, in fact, a fragment of silver-bearing quartz — the zig-zag thread of blue which ran like a vein across the broken edge betrayed its quality to Nevins at a glance.

A week after this it was noised through Red Rock that a party from New England had struck a silver lode of surprising richness farther up the valley. That night John Dent wrote a long letter to Prudence. Three nights afterwards the Road Agents overhauled the Walla Walla Express, and the gutted mail-bag was thrown into a swamp.

Perhaps there was more truth than jest in Mr. Dent's picture of the Bannock chieftains puzzling over the rhetoric of Jack's epistle.

John Dent's visions of wealth would have been realized in a few months, but unfortunately the silver lode, as if repenting its burst of generosity, abruptly turned coy, and refused to lavish any more favors. Just when their shaft was piercing deeper and deeper into the earth, and their rock growing richer and richer — just as they had fallen into a haughty habit of looking upon one another as millionaires — the lode began to narrow. It was six feet wide when it began to narrow; from that point it narrowed relentlessly day by day for a fortnight, and then was a thin seam like a knife-blade — then "pinched out" and utterly disappeared. After four weeks of drifting, and shafting, and all manner of prospecting, they failed to find it again, and gave up. Some said it was only a rich "chamber;" some said it was one of those treacherous "pockets;" and some said it was a good "chimney," and was down there yet, somewhere: but whatever its name or its nature might be, Dent, Nevins, and Twombly recognized the fact that it had got away from them, and that was the main grievance.

"Anyhow, we have made a fair haul," remarked Nevins, "thanks to you, Jack, for it was you who lighted on the thing."

"My luck is your luck and Twombly's," Dent replied.

They had, as Nevins stated, made a fair haul. They had managed to get out close upon a thousand tons of forty-dollar rock before the calamity came, and after all expenses of mining and crushing were paid, they found themselves nearly thirty thousand dollars in pocket.

Their pile was so large now — they had reduced it to greenbacks which they concealed on the premises — and its reputation so much exaggerated, that they took turns in guarding the tent, only two going to work at a time. The presence of thieves in the camp had been successfully demonstrated within the month, and the fear of being robbed settled upon them like a nightmare. Dent had another apprehension, the coming of the cold season. Nevins reassured him on that point. Though the winter was severe in Montana, they were in a sheltered valley; at the worst there could be only a few weeks when they could not work.

The silver exhausted, they fell to prospecting. After varying fortunes for a fortnight, they had another find, Twombly being the involuntary Columbus. It was gold on this occasion, and though it did not yield so bounteously as the silver lode, it panned out handsomely.

So the weeks wore away, and the young men saw their store steadily increasing day by day. It was heart-breaking work sometimes, and back-breaking work always; but it was the kind of work that makes a man willing to have his back, if not his heart, broken.

The winter which Dent had looked forward to so apprehensively was over, and had been propitious to the gold-hunters. Spring-time again filled the valley to the very brim with color and perfume, as a goblet is filled with wine. Then the long summer set in.

All this while John Dent had refrained from writing home; it was his design to take Prudence and his uncle by surprise, by walking unheralded into Willowbrook some happy day, with his treasures.

Those treasures had become a heavy care to the young men. "We keep the dust" — I am quoting from the journal — "in a stout candle-box set into the earth at the foot of the tent-pole, and one of us lies across it at night. There have been two attempts to rob us. The other night Joe turned over in his sleep, and found himself clutching a man by the leg. An empty boot was left in his hand, and a black figure darted out of the tent. There was a search the next morning for that other boot. There were plenty of men with two boots, and not a few with none at all; but the man with one boot was wanting, and well for him! If he had been caught it would have been death on the spot; the blackest scoundrels in camp would have assisted at his execution, for there's nothing so disgusts knaves as a crime of this sort — when they have n't a finger in it themselves."

The morning after this attempt at burglary — it was the second — the following conversation took place —

"It will never do for us to keep all this dust here," said Nevins; "we can't hide it as cunningly as we do the greenbacks."

"What can we do with it?" asked John Dent.

"There's an agent here of Tileston & Co.'s who will give us drafts on Salt Lake City, or turn it into bank-notes at a Jewish discount."

Dent and Twombly preferred the bank-notes.

"Drafts would be safer," suggested Nevins.
"Suppose Tileston & Co. should fail?"
"That is true, again," observed Nevins.

The bank-notes were decided on, and forty-five slips of crisp paper in all, each with an adorable M on it, were shut up in a leather pocket-book, which they buried in the middle of the tent, piling their saddles over the hiding-place.

They had now been nearly twelve months at the diggings, and John Dent's share in the property reached five figures. It was not the wealth of his dreams; every day in Wall Street men make three times as much by a scratch of the pen; but it was enough to set him on his feet. With fifteen thousand dollars in his pocket he could ask Prudence Palfrey to marry him. Red Rock was overrun, and the supply of metal giving out. If he remained without lighting on fresh finds, what he had would melt away like snow in the March sunshine. Was it worth while to tempt fortune further? was it likely that two such golden windfalls would happen to the same mortal? He put these questions to Nevins and Twombly, who were aware of the stress that drew him to New England. They knew his love-affair by heart, and had even seen a certain small photograph which John Dent had brought with him from Rivermouth.

Nevins declared his own intention to hold on by Red Rock. Twombly was for instantly returning home. With fifteen thousand dollars in the Nautilus Bank at Rivermouth, he would snap his fingers at Count Monte Cristo himself, who, by the way, was as real a personage to Twombly as John Jacob Astor. The two New England men decided to join the next large party that started for the East.

The incalculable sums which our friends were imagined to have accumulated rendered their position critical. They took turns regularly on the night-watch now, and waited with increasing apprehension and impatience for the making up of a train to cross the mountains.

Red Rock had not improved with time. It seethed and bubbled, like a witch's caldron, with all evil passions. Men who might have been decently honest if they had been decently fortunate, turned knaves. Crowds of successful diggers had already shaken the gold-dust from their feet and departed; only the dissolute and the vicious remained, with here and there a luckless devil who could not get away. The new-comers, and there were throngs of them, were of the worst description. Every man carried his life in his hand, and did not seem to value it highly. It was suicide to stray beyond the limits of the town after dusk. Tents were plundered every night. Now, though murder did not shock the nerves of this community, the thieving did. An attempt was made by indignant citizens of Red Rock to put a stop to that. They went so far as to suspend from the bough of a butternut-tree one of their most influential townsmen, a gentleman known as the Great American Pie-Eater (on account of certain gastronomic feats performed at Salt Lake City), but the proceeding met with so little popular favor, that the culprit was taken down and resuscitated and invited by his executioners to stand drinks all round at Gallagher's bar — which he did.

When the Vigilantes sprung into existence, they managed these things differently in Montana: they did not take their man down so soon, for one thing.

"If we had been there by ourselves," said Joseph Twombly, describing Red Rock at this period, "we'd have been murdered in less than a week." But there was, it seemed, something about Nevins that had a depressing effect upon the spirits of sundry volatile gentlemen in camp.

One morning just before daybreak, John Dent awoke suddenly and sat up in his blankets, trembling from head to foot. At what he did not know. He had not been dreaming, and it was not a noise that had broken his sleep. He looked about him; every object stood out clearly in the twilight; Twombly lay snoring in his shake-down, but Nevins, whose watch it was, was not in the tent. Dent was somehow struck cold by that. He rolled out of the blankets, and crawling over to the spot where the money was hidden, felt for it under the saddles. The earth around the place had been newly turned up, and THE POCKET-BOOK WAS GONE!

The pocket-book was gone, and one of the three saddles — Nevins's — was missing. The story told itself. The outcries of the two men brought a crowd of diggers to the tent.

"We have been robbed by our partner!" cried Twombly, picking up a saddle by the stirrup-strap and hurrying out to the corral for his horse.

John Dent lay on the ground with his finger-nails buried in the loose earth near the empty hole. A couple of worthies, half roughly and half compassionately, set him upon his feet.

"Do you care to know who that mate of yours was?"

The speaker was a gaunt, sunburnt man, with deer-skin leggins, fringed at the seams and gathered at the waist by a U. S. belt, from which hung the inevitable bowie-knife and revolver. Dent looked at him stupidly, and dimly recognized one of the two miners who had disputed the claim with Nevins that first 'afternoon in camp.

"I knew he'd levant with the pile, some day. But I didn't like to let on, for fear of mistakes. I thought, may be, you other two was the same kind. I knew that man in Tuolumne County. He's a devil. He's the only man breathing I'm afraid of. No, I don't mind allowing I'm afraid of him. There's something about him, when I think of it — a sort of cold cheek — so that I'd rather meet a Bannock war-party in a narrer gully than have any unpleasantness with that man. His true name wasn't Dick King, I reckon, because he said it was. Cool Dick was what they called him in Tuolumne County in '56."

Several ears in the crowd pricked up at the words Cool Dick. It was a pseudonym rather well known on the Pacific slope. John Dent had recovered his senses by this.

"Are there any true lads here," he cried, "that will go with me to bring back that thief?"

A dozen volunteered at once, and half an hour later twenty armed men galloped out of Red Rock Cañon.

They returned with jaded horses, at sunset, without having struck the trail of either Twombly or Nevins. The next day, at noon, Twombly himself rode into camp and dropped heavily out of the saddle at the door of the tent. He had a charge of buckshot in his leg. Some one had fired on him from the chaparral near Big Hole Ranch. It was not Nevins, for he had no gun, so far as known; probably some confederate of his.

And this was the end of it. This was the result of their twelve months' hardship and industry and pluck and endurance.

Then John Dent wrote that letter to Prudence, which she laid away in the drawer, telling her the story, not as I have told it, tamely and at second-hand, but with fire and tears. Then, in a few weeks, came Joseph Twombly, limping back into Rivermouth, alone. There were no more El Dorados for him, poor knight; he was lamed for life, or he would never have deserted his comrade. John Dent himself had gone off, Twombly did not know where; but to California, he fancied, in search of George Nevins.

And this was the end of it for Prudence, too. She shut up the letter and her dream in the writing-desk with the brass clamps. It was a year before she could read the letter without a recurrence of the old poignant pain. At the end of another twelvemonth, when she unfolded the pages, the words wore a strange, faded look, as if they had been written by one long ago dead, and dealt only with dimly remembered events and persons — so far off seemed that summer morning when she first read them. She shed no tears now, but held the letter in her hand thoughtfully.

It was nearly three years since John Dent went away from Rivermouth, and nothing more had been heard of him. A silence like and unlike that of the grave had gathered about his name. Life at Willowbrook flowed back into its accustomed channels. Mr. Dent had disposed of the skeleton effectively and forever, and Prudence had passed into the early summer of her womanhood. It was at this point my chronicle began.

This was the situation — to borrow a technical term from dramatic art — when the congregation of the Old Brick Church, after much ruffling of parochial plumage, resolved to relieve Parson Wibird Hawkins of his pastorate.

VIII

THE PARSON'S LAST TEXT

This brings my story again to that afternoon in May, when Prudence Palfrey made her appearance at the cottage in Horseshoe Lane, and was solicited by Salome to speak to the parson, who had locked himself in the little room after the departure of the two deacons.

It was with an inexplicable sense of uneasiness that Prudence crossed the library, and knocked softly on the panel of the inner door. The parson did not seem to hear the summons; at all events, he paid no attention to it, and Prudence knocked again.

"He's gittin' the least bit hard of hearin', pore soul," said Salome. "Mebbe he heard that, though," she added more cautiously, "for he always hears when you don't s'pose he will. Do jest speak to him, honey; he'll know your vice in a minit."

Prudence put her lips down to the keyhole and called, "Parson Wibird! — it's Prue — won't you speak to me?"

He made no response to this, and in the silence that ensued, broken only by the quick respiration of the two women, there was no sound as if he were preparing to undo the fastenings. Prudence rose up with a half-frightened expression on her countenance and looked at Salome.

"What can have happened?" she said hurriedly.

"Lord o' mercy knows," replied Salome, catching Prue's alarm. "Don't stare at me in sech a way, dear; I'm as nervous as nuthin'."

"Are you sure he is there?"

"Sartin. I all but see him goin' in, an' I haven't ben out of the room sence. He must be there."

"Is he subject to vertigo, ever?"

"Dunno," said Salome doubtfully.

"I mean, does he ever faint?"

"He did have a cur'ous sort of spell two or three weeks ago, an' Dr. Theophilus give him some med'cine for it."

"He has fainted, then! Get a candle — quick. Stop, Salome, I'll go with you."

Prudence was afraid to remain in the library alone. She was impressed by some impalpable presence in the half darkness. The shadows huddled together in the corners. The long rows of books in their time-stained leather bindings looked down sombrely from the shelves. On the table was an open volume, with a paper-cutter upon it, which the parson had been reading. His frayed dressing-gown lay across a chair in front of the table. It seemed like some weird, collapsed figure, lying there. All the familiar objects in the room had turned strange and woe-begone in the twilight. Prudence would not have been left alone for the world.

The two went out together for the candle, which Salome with a trembling hand lighted at the kitchen stove. Then they flitted back to the library silently, with white sharp faces, like ghosts.

"What shall we do?"

"We must break in the door," said Prudence under her breath. "You hold the candle."

She placed her knee against the lower panel and pressed with all her strength. The lock was old and rusty, and the screws worked loosely in the worm-eaten wood-work. The door yielded at the second pressure and flew open, with a shower of fine dust sifting down from the lintel.

The girl retreated a step or two, and shading her eyes with the palm of her hand, peered into the darkened space.

Nothing was distinct at first, but as Salome raised the light above Prue's head, the figure of the parson suddenly took shape against the gloom.

He was sitting in an old-fashioned arm-chair, with his serene face bent over a great Bible covered with green baize, which he held on his knees. His left arm hung idly at his side, and the forefinger of his right hand rested lightly on the middle of the page, as if slumber had overtaken him so, reading.

"Laws o' mercy, if the parson has n't gone to sleep!" exclaimed Salome, stepping into the small compartment.

"Asleep!" repeated Prudence, the reassured color returning to her cheek.

Salome laid her hand on the parson's arm, and then passed it quickly over his forehead.

"He's dead!" cried Salome, dropping the candlestick.

The hour-hand of the cuckoo-clock in the hall at Willowbrook pointed at seven; the toy bird popped out on the narrow ledge in front of the carved Swiss cottage, shook seven flute-like notes into the air, popped in again hastily, and the little door went to with a spiteful snap.

Mr. Dent glanced at the timepiece over the

The figure of the parson suddenly took shape

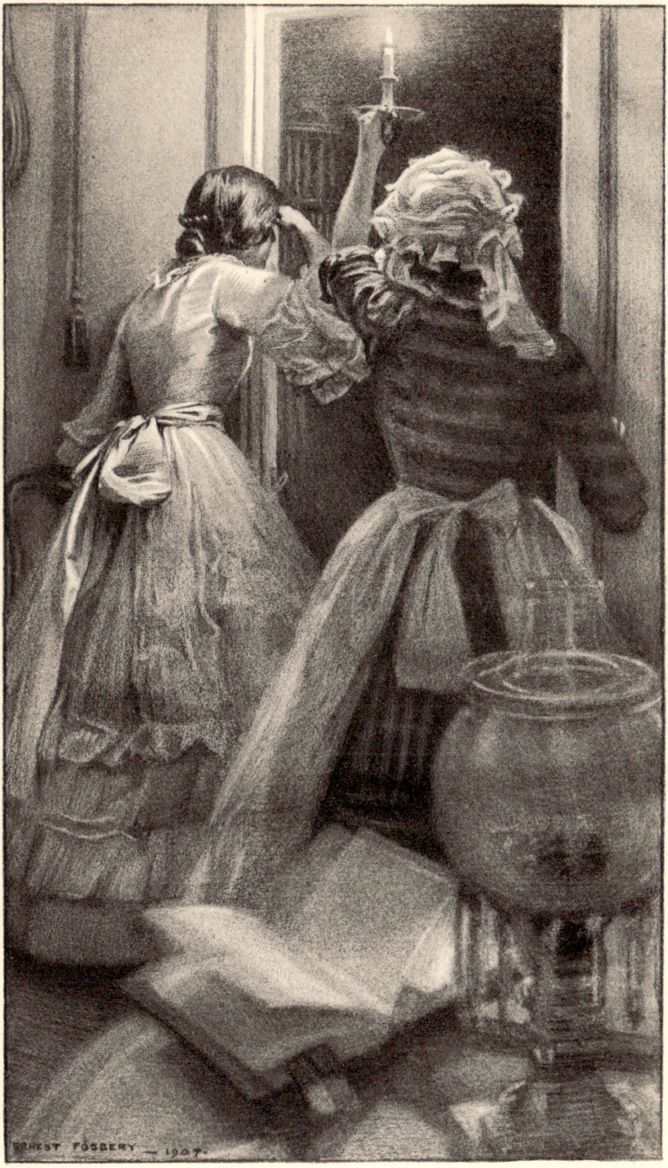
ERNEST FOSBERY — 1907.

PRUDENCE PALFREY 117

fireplace in the sitting-room, and wondered what was detaining Prue. She had gone to town on a shopping expedition shortly after dinner, and here it was an hour and a half past tea-time. Fanny had brought in the tea-urn and carried it off again. It was as if the sun-dial had forgotten to mark the movements of the sun; the household set its clocks by Prudence.

For the last hour or two Mr. Dent had been lounging restlessly in the sitting-room, now snatching up a book and trying to read, now looking out on the lawn, and now vigorously poking the coals in the grate, for it was one of those brisk days which make a fire comfortable in our delusive New England May.

Mr. Dent was revolving in his mind how he should break to Prudence the intelligence of Parson Hawkins's dismissal, and more especially in what terms he should confess his own part in the transaction. "What will Prue say?" was a question he put to himself a dozen times without eliciting a satisfactory reply. He was a little afraid of Prudence — he had that tender awe of her with which a pure woman inspires most men. He could imagine what she would have said three years ago; but she had altered in many respects since then; she had grown quieter and less impulsive.

That one flurry of passion in which she had confessed her love for John Dent did not seem credible to her guardian as he looked back to it. As a matter of course, she would be indignant at the action of the deacons, and would probably not approve of the steps he had taken to bring Mr. Dillingham to Rivermouth; but she would not storm at him. He almost wished she would storm at him, for her anger was not so unmanageable as the look of mute reproach which she knew how to bring into her gray eyes.

The cuckoo in the Swiss chalet had hopped out again on the ledge, and was just sounding the half-hour in his clear, business-like way, when Prudence opened the drawing-room door.

"I thought you had run off for good," said Mr. Dent, rising from his chair; then he stopped and looked at her attentively. "Why, Prue, what is the matter?"

"The parson" — Prudence could not finish the sentence. The nervous strength that had sustained her through the recent ordeal gave way; she sank upon the sofa and buried her face in the cushions.

"She has heard of it already," thought Mr. Dent. He crossed to the sofa and rested his hand softly on her shoulder. "My dear girl, you must be reasonable. It had to come sooner or later ; he could not go on preaching forever, you know. He is a very old man now, and ought to take his ease. He will be all the happier with the cares of the parish off his hands."

"All the happier, yes!"

"And we'll have him up to Willowbrook often ; he shall have a room here" —

Prudence lifted her face beseechingly.

"Oh, you don't know! you don't know!" she cried. "He is dead! he died this afternoon, sitting in his chair. Ah! — it was so dreadfully sudden!" And Prudence covered her eyes with her hands as if to shut out the scene in the library.

Mr. Dent was greatly shocked. He leaned against the mantelpiece, and stared vacantly at Prudence, while she related what had happened at Horseshoe Lane. She had completed her purchases in town, and was on the way home when she met Miss Blydenburgh, who told her of the deacons' visit to Parson Hawkins to request his resignation. Knowing that the poor old man was unprepared for any such proposition, she had turned back and hastened down to the parsonage, to say and do what she could to comfort him in his probable distress. Then she and Salome, alone there in the dark, had found him dead in the chair.

Mr. Dent left his tea untasted. He had the horse saddled, and rode over to town. He was greatly shocked. And Deacon Zeb Twombly, that night, as he stood for a moment beside the cradle in which the little ewe-lamb lay nestled in its blankets, was a miserable man. He crept off to the spare room in the attic — where he was undergoing a temporary but not unprecedented exile — with the conviction that he was little better than a murderer.

"I hope Parson Wibird will forgive me my share in the business," murmured the deacon, blowing out the candle; then he lingered by the window dejectedly. It was a dreamy May night; the air, though chilly, was full of the odors of spring, and the mysterious blue spaces above were sown thick with stars. "P'rhaps he knows all up there," he said, lifting his eyes reverently, "an' how it went agin me to give him any pain. I wonder how brother Wendell feels about it."

Deacon Wendell, fortunately or unfortunately, as the case may be, was of that tougher fibre out of which the strong sons of the world are made. He had performed the duty that devolved upon him, as he had performed other unpleasant duties, having been sheriff once, and there was nothing to be said. He was sorry the parson died just as he did. "Looks as though he done it on purpose to spite us," reflected Deacon Wendell. Perhaps his chief emotion when he first heard the news — it was all over Rivermouth now — was an ill-defined feeling of resentment against Parson Wibird for having cut up rough.

The effect produced on Mr. Dent was more complex. Though neither so callous as Deacon Wendell nor so soft-hearted as Deacon Twombly, he shared to some extent the feelings of both. He keenly regretted the death of the old parson, and particularly the manner of it. It was an unlucky coincidence — he could not look upon it as anything more than a coincidence — and would give rise to much disagreeable gossip. If it had happened a month or two before, or a month or two later, he would have been sorry, as anybody is sorry when anybody dies; but he would not have been shocked. He wished he had not been quite so warm in advocating the desirableness of Mr. Dillingham. If he could have foreseen the present catastrophe, he would have thrust his hand into the flames rather than move in the matter.

But what was done was done; and as he urged the mare across the long wooden bridge which ended among the crumbling wharves and shabby warehouses of Market Street, he trusted something would transpire showing that the parson's death was the result of natural causes and in no degree to be attributed to — to what had probably caused it.

There was an unusual glimmer and moving of lights in the windows of the parsonage, and a mysterious coming and going of shadows on the brown Holland shades, as Mr. Dent turned into Horseshoe Lane. He was within a dozen rods of the cottage, when the gate creaked on its hinges and Dr. Theophilus Tredick passed out, walking off rapidly in an opposite direction.

Mr. Dent pushed on after the doctor, and overtook him at the doorstep of a neighboring house.

"A moment, Doctor," said Mr. Dent, leaning over the horse's neck. "Has there been an inquest?"

"Yes; we have just finished the examination."

"Well?"

"Paralysis."

"Attributable to any sudden mental excitement or anything of that nature? You know he had a conversation on church affairs with the deacons this afternoon; could that have affected him in any way?" Mr. Dent put the query anxiously.

"It would be difficult to say," replied the doctor. "It is open to conjecture of course; but at the worst it could only have hastened what was inevitable. I am not prepared to affirm that it hastened it; in fact, I do not think it did."

"I do not entirely catch your meaning, Doctor," Mr. Dent said.

"I mean that Parson Hawkins had had two slight strokes of paralysis previously; one last winter and the second three weeks ago. I was apprehensive that the third would terminate fatally."

"I never heard of that."

"No one knew of it, I think; not even Mrs. Pinder, the housekeeper. It was at his own urgent request I kept the matter secret. At the time of the occurrence of the second attack I had a long talk with our friend, and advised him strongly to give up work altogether; finding him obstinate on that point, I urged him to have an assistant. I warned him plainly that he might be taken ill at any moment in the pulpit. He declared that that was the place of all others where he could wish to die; but he promised to consider my suggestion of an associate minister."

"Which he never did."

"For the last three Sundays," continued the

doctor, "I have gone to church expecting to see him drop down in the pulpit in the midst of the service. He was aware of his condition, and not at all alarmed by it. Though he overrated his strength, and had some odd notions of duty — he did have some odd notions, our estimable old friend — he was a man of great clear sense, and I do not believe the recent action of the parish affected him in the manner or to the extent idle persons will suppose. What has happened would probably have happened in any case."

Dr. Tredick's statement lifted a weight from Mr. Dent's bosom, and from Deacon Twombly's when he heard of it; though there were numerous persons in the town who did not hesitate to assert that the parson's dismissal killed him. To look on the darkest side of a picture is in strict keeping with the local spirit; for Rivermouth, in its shortcomings and in its uncompromising virtues, is nothing if not Puritan.

"Might as well have took a muskit and shot the ole man," observed Mr. Wiggins.

"Capital punishment ought to be abolished in New Hampshire," said ex-postmaster Snelling, "if they don't hang Deacon Wendell and the rest of 'em."

Mr. Snelling was not naturally a sanguinary person, but he had been superseded in the post-office the year before by Deacon Wendell, and flesh is flesh.

The event was the only topic discussed for the next ten days. Parson Wibird had so long been one of the features of the place, that he seemed a permanence, like the Brick Church itself, or the post-office with its granite façade. If either of these had been spirited off over night, the surprise and the shock could not have been more wide-spread. That tall, stooping figure, clad always in a rusty suit of black, was as familiar an object on the main street as the swinging sign of the Old Bell Tavern. There were grandfathers and grandmothers who, as boys and girls, remembered Parson Wibird when he looked neither older nor younger than he did that day lying in the coffin — nay, not so young, for the deep wrinkles and scars of time had faded out of the kindly old face, and the radiance of heavenly youth rested upon it.

There was one circumstance connected with the old minister's death that naturally made a deeper impression than any other. When Salome summoned the neighbors, that night, they found the parson with the Bible lying open before him, and one finger resting upon the page as if directing attention to a particular passage. There was something startlingly life-like and imperative in the unconscious pointing of that withered forefinger, and those who peered hastily over the slanted shoulder and read the verse indicated never forgot it.

"Thet was th' parson's las' tex'," said Uncle Jedd, leaning on his spade worn bright with oh! so many graves: "Well done, thou good an' faithful servant, enter thou inter th' joy of thy Lord!"

IX

A WILL, AND THE WAY OF IT

It was early in the forenoon, six or seven days after the funeral of the parson, that Mr. Dent, who had left the house an hour before to take the morning train for Boston, returned hurriedly to Willowbrook, and, capturing Fanny the housemaid, with broom and dust-pan in the front hall, despatched her to her mistress.

"Tell Miss Prudence I want to speak with her a moment in the library."

This change in her guardian's purpose, and his message, which was in itself something out of the ordinary way, filled Prudence with wonder. She had packed Mr. Dent's valise for an absence of several days, and she knew it was no trivial circumstance that had made him relinquish or postpone the journey in question. What could it be?

She was arranging the house-plants in the bay-window room, as it was called, when Fanny delivered Mr. Dent's message.

"He must have missed the train," said Prudence to herself. But Mr. Dent had gone to town an hour earlier than was necessary to catch the express. "Or perhaps Mr. Dillingham has written that he is not coming, after all." Suddenly an idea flashed upon Prudence and nearly caused her to drop the pot of jonquils which she was in the act of lifting from the flower-stand.

"He has heard from John Dent!"

When a friend dies and is buried, that is the end of him. We miss him for a space out of our daily existence; we mourn for him by degrees that become mercifully less; we cling to the blessed hope that we shall be reunited in some more perfect sphere; but so far as this earth is concerned, that is the end of him. However near and dear he was, the time arrives when he does not form a part of our daily thought; he ceases to be even an abstraction. We go no more with flowers and tears into the quiet cemetery; only the rain and the snow-flakes fall there; we leave it for the fingers of Spring to deck the neglected mound.

But when our friend vanishes unaccountably in the midst of a crowded city, or goes off on a sea-voyage and is never heard of again, his memory has a singular tenacity. He may be to all intents and purposes dead to us, but we have not lost him. The ring of the door-bell at midnight may be his ring; the approaching footstep may be his footstep; the unexpected letter with foreign postmark may be from his hand. He haunts us as the dead never can.

The woman whose husband died last night may marry again within a lustre of months. Do you suppose a week passes by when the woman whose husband disappeared mysteriously ten years ago does not think of him? There are moments when the opening of a door must startle her.

There is no real absence but death.

For nearly three years, for two years and a half, to be precise, the shadow of John Dent had haunted Prudence more or less — the chance of tidings from him, the possibility of his emerging suddenly from the darkness that shrouded him and his movements, had been in her thought almost constantly. Until she saw him once more or knew that he was dead, she was not to be relieved of this sense of expectancy. It was disassociated with any idea or desire that he would claim her love; he had surrendered that; he had written her that he should never set foot in Rivermouth again; he was a wrecked man. It was not for Prudence to cling to a hope which he had thrown over, however unwisely or weakly. She would have waited for him loyally all her life; his misfortune would have linked her closer to him ; but he had not asked her to wait, or to share the misfortune ; he had given her up, and the obvious thing for Prudence had been to forget him. In a circumscribed life like hers, how was it possible for her to forget that she had loved and been loved? She taught herself to look upon his visit to Willowbrook, and what had subsequently occurred, as a midsummer's day-dream ; but beyond that she had not been successful.

John Dent's name was seldom spoken now either by Prudence or her guardian ; to all appearance he was obliterated from their memories ; but the truth is, there was scarcely a month when both Prudence and Mr. Dent did not wonder what had become of him. "I don't believe she ever thinks of him nowadays," reflected Mr. Dent. "He has quite forgotten him," Prudence would say to herself. But Mr. Dent never took his letters from the languid clerk at the post-office without half expecting to find one from Jack ; and Prudence never caught an expression more than usually thoughtful on her guardian's face without fancying he had received news of his nephew.

The image of John Dent rose up before Prudence with strange distinctness that morning as she stood by the bay-window, and flitted with singular persistence across her path on the way down-stairs.

Mr. Dent was seated at the library table, upon which were spread several legal-looking documents with imposing red-wax seals. His eyebrows were drawn together, and there was a perplexed look on his countenance which at once reassured Prudence; whatever had occurred, it was nothing tragic.

"We have got hold of the parson's will at last," he said, looking up as she entered the room.

A will had been found the day following Parson Hawkins's death, in an old hair-trunk in which he kept private papers; but Mr. Jarvis, the attorney, declared that a later testament had been executed, different in tenor from this, which was dated fifteen years back. No such document was forthcoming, however, after a most rigorous search among the old clergyman's manuscripts. Mr. Jarvis had drawn up the paper himself ten months before, and was bent on finding it.

"My client was queer in such matters," he said. "He would keep scraps of verse and paragraphs cut from newspapers in his strong-box at the bank, and have bonds and leases lying around the library as if they were worthless. You may depend upon it, he stuck this will away in some corner, and forgot it."

On the sixth or seventh day, when the belief was become general that the parson had destroyed it, the later will was discovered shut up in a copy of the London folio edition of Cotton Mather's Magnalia, on a shelf in the little room where the parson had died.

"He has left Salome a life-interest in the cottage and an annual sum for her support, to revert at her death to the main estate."

"I am glad of that," said Prudence. "Poor Salome!"

"And the residue of the property," continued Mr. Dent, "after deducting a few minor bequests — how do you think he has disposed of that?"

"I am sure I cannot imagine. He had no near relatives. To the Sunday-school, perhaps."

"No."

"To the Brick Church, then."

"No."

"To the Mariners' Home."

"No; the Mariners' Home gets two thousand dollars, though."

"Then I cannot guess."

"He leaves it to John Dent," said her guardian, with a curious smile, watching Prudence narrowly as he spoke the words.

"Isn't that rather singular?" said Prudence, without ruffling a feather.

"She does n't care the snap of her finger for him, that is certain," was Mr. Dent's internal comment. — "No, not singular. My brother Benjamin and Parson Hawkins were close friends for many years. I believe Benjamin helped him in some money affair when they were at college together, and his gratitude is not unnatural — assuming that gratitude is a great deal more common than it is. But the injunction laid upon the executors — and I am one — *is* singular. The executors are not to settle up the estate, and Jack is not to be informed of his inheritance — provided we could find him — until a year after the death of the testator."

"What a strange provision!"

"The parson explains it by saying that every man ought to earn his own living; that sudden wealth is frequently the worst misfortune that can befall a young man, and he wishes his friend's son to rely on his own exertions for a while, 'in order' — and these are the parson's very words — 'that he may learn to estimate riches at their proper value, and support prosperity without arrogance.' All of which is sensible enough, and quite in the style of your friend Dr. Johnson, but rather odd on the whole. Indeed, the will is as angular as one of the parson's sermons. Jarvis drew it up, but he could not have composed a sentence of it to save him. Anyway, Jack falls heir to a round sum — about eighty thousand dollars, not including the house and lot in Horseshoe Lane."

"And perhaps at this moment he is without bread to eat, or a roof to shelter him!"

"Most likely. He has not condescended to let his friends know what he has done with himself. But as you said long ago, it will be a great thing for him; it will teach him self-reliance. I did n't think then he needed any lessons in that branch of science; but I have altered my opinion. It was cowardly in Jack to strike his colors at the first fire. I was mistaken and disappointed in him. I suppose it is the fellow's pride that has kept him from writing to me."

"I am sure something ought to be done about him now, uncle."

"If I knew what to do. I could not tell him of Parson Hawkins's will, if he were here. I don't imagine an advertisement in the papers would be a very tempting bait to Jack. Letters have no effect on him, apparently. When I saw you so unhap— I mean when we got the story of that rascally Nevins, I wrote Jack to come home and take a fresh start; offered to organize a mining company, make him superintendent, and go into the business in a rational manner; but he never answered my letter, if he got it."

"That was very generous of you," said Prudence, to whom this was news.

"I don't like his silence. Why, it is two years and a half, going on three years. Sometimes, you know, I fancy he has fallen in with that man, and come to harm. The idea may have passed through the parson's mind also, which would account for the surprising codicil he added to the will."

The subject of the will and all connected with it was painful to Prudence, but she was instantly curious to know what this surprising codicil was, and said so in that involuntary language which belongs to expressive eyes.

Mr. Dent took up one of the solemn-looking documents and glanced at the last page, then laid it down, then turned to it again, and re-read a certain passage deliberately, as if to assure himself before he spoke.

"In case of John Dent's death," he said, "in case he dies within the twelve months specified, the property comes to *you*."

"No, no! it must never come to me!" cried Prudence, starting from the great armchair in which she had curled herself. "He must be found; whether he is told of it or not, he must be found!"

"I think myself he ought to be looked up. It is ridiculous for him to be roughing it out there — wherever he is — with all this money coming to him in a few months. But it is not clear to me what can be done about it."

"Cannot some one be sent to find him? Joseph Twombly, for instance?"

"Yes, Twombly might be sent; and get some buckshot in that other leg — his luck. He would go in a second if it were suggested; but Twombly has just secured a good situation in Chicago — did n't I mention it to you? — and I am not sure I should be justified in asking him."

Joseph Twombly, ex-knight and capitalist, had bowed gracefully and good-humoredly to fate, instead of throwing up his hands and rending his garments, like his disconsolate leader. For many months after his return from El Dorado, the good knight could get nothing to do, and in truth he was not capable of doing much, on account of his wound. He lay idle around Rivermouth, to the no slight embarrassment of Deacon Twombly, who was not prospering in a worldly point of view. Ewe-lambs had become chronic in the deacon's family, and he found himself again banished, as the reader has been informed, to the spare room in the attic, and a new lamb had come to be fed even before the little one of a previous season was fairly upon its mottled legs. It was at this time — two weeks before Parson Hawkins's fatal stroke of paralysis, and while Mr. Dent was urging his friend Dillingham to consider the Rivermouth proposal — that a piece of sunny fortune fell to the portion of Joseph Twombly.

Mr. Dent was not a man who unbosomed himself to every chance acquaintance, but he had been particularly communicative with Mr. Dillingham touching Rivermouth affairs, and had not left untold the history of his nephew's misfortunes. I am inclined to suspect, however, that Mr. Dent restricted himself to the financial parts of the narrative, and said nothing whatever of the trifling love-passage that had taken place between his ward and John Dent. It would have been hardly fair to Prudence to speak of that; but he talked frequently of his nephew, all the more frequently, perhaps, because the subject was tabooed at home. It chanced one evening, as the two gentlemen were chatting together in a private parlor at the Astor House, that the conversation turned on Twombly.

"I am afraid Joseph is a heavy burden to the deacon, just now," Mr. Dent said. "I wish I could help the fellow; but every one is retrenching on account of the troubles down

South, and there seems to be no opening for Joseph."

"He appears to be an estimable and faithful young person," Mr. Dillingham replied, "and I should take it as a favor if I might be allowed to join you in any plan to assist him. I have no business influence here, but I am confident that a word from me to my Chicago bankers would secure interest for Mr. Twombly there. Suppose I write to them?"

Mr. Dillingham did write, and Messrs. Rawlings & Sons were pleased to find a place in their office for a young man so highly spoken of by their esteemed correspondent. A few days afterwards Mr. Joseph Twombly, with a comfortable check in his pocket, was on his way to Chicago.

To recall him now, and send him on a wild-goose chase after John Dent, was a step not to be taken without consideration, if at all.

"He is out of the question at present. Perhaps by and by, if I fail to obtain any clue to Jack's whereabouts, I may be forced to make use of Joseph. What was the name of that banking firm at Salt Lake City which Jack mentioned in his letter? Look it up, and I will write to those people."

"It was Tileston & Co.," replied Prudence, who had an excellent memory.

"And I'll write to Jack also at Red Rock — the rock on which he split," supplemented Mr. Dent; but his little pleasantry fell cold. Prudence was not in a mood to encourage jests, and Mr. Dent withdrew crestfallen into his serious shell. "Perhaps it would be advisable to drop him a line at San Francisco," he said. "What do you think?"

Mr. Dent went to work on his letters, and Prudence stole off thoughtfully to the small bay-window room over the hall door, where she always did her meditating. This business of the will weighed heavily upon her. There was something chilling in the reflection that possibly the dead man had left his money to a dead man, and it would thus fall to her — an avalanche of clammy gold-pieces slipping through dead men's fingers! She would touch none of it! The idea made her shiver.

She was still sitting by the open casement, dismayed at the prospect, when Mr. Dent stepped out of the door below, a valise in his hand, and his spring overcoat thrown across one arm.

Prudence drew back hastily, and when Mr. Dent looked up at the window, she was not visible. The movement had been mechanical on her part, and she was instantly ashamed of it. Of course it was perfectly proper that her guardian should meet the Rev. Mr. Dillingham in Boston, and conduct him to Rivermouth; Mr. Dent was in a manner bound to so much courtesy; but the thought of a stranger standing in the dear old parson's pulpit brought the tears to Prudence's eyes.

"It is very uncharitable and unchristian, I know," said Prudence, watching her guardian's receding figure, "but I think I shall hate the new minister."

X

THE NEW MINISTER

RIVERMOUTH is a town where almost literally nothing happens. Sometimes somebody is married, and sometimes somebody dies — with surprising abruptness, as the old parson did, for example — and sometimes a vessel is blown on the rocks at the mouth of the harbor. But of those salient tragedies and comedies which make up the sum of life in cities, Rivermouth knows next to nothing. Since the hanging of a witch or two in the pre-Revolutionary days, the office of sheriff there has been virtually a sinecure. The police-court — where now and then a thoughtless, light-fingered person is admonished of the error of his ways, and the one habitual drunkard is periodically despatched to the Town-Farm — seems almost like a branch of the Sunday-school. The community may be said to have lived for thirty years on a single divorce case, growing out of the elopement of Major Tom Deering with Mrs. Honoria Maddox — to this day a perilous story

> "That matrons tell, with sharpened tongue,
> To maids with downcast eyes."

In default of great events, small matters rise to the first magnitude in Rivermouth. There are persons there who can give you, if you chance to be to the manner born, the most minute particulars of the career of your great-grandfather, and to whom what you have for dinner is far from being an uninteresting item.

"I see Cappen Chris Bell at Seth Wiggins's this mornin'," says Mr. Uriah Stebbens to Mr. Caleb Stokels; "he bought that great turkey of Seth's, and six poun's of steak — right off the tenderline. Guess he expects his brother-in-law's family down from Bostin. Cappen Chris Bell always was a good provider."

This piece of information lies like a live coal upon the brain of Mr. Stokels until, with becoming gravity, he turns it over to some other inquiring neighbor. At a moderate estimate, not less than two thirds of the entire population of Rivermouth sit down in imagination at Captain Christopher Bell's dinner-table the next day.

Unless the reader is familiar with the interior life of secluded New England towns like Rivermouth, he will find it difficult to understand the excitement that prevailed on the Sunday when the Rev. Mr. James Dillingham preached his first sermon in the Old Brick Church. Yet even a stranger, passing through the streets, crowded at the earliest stroke of the bells — I think there is no music this side of heaven sweeter than the clangor of those same Rivermouth bells — could not have failed to notice an unwonted, eager look on the faces of the neatly dressed throng. There was something in the very atmosphere different from that of ordinary days. A sort of pious Fourth-of-July halo diffused itself through the fleecy, low-hanging clouds, which, with May-time capriciousness, broke into fine rain before the service was concluded. A circumstance in which Uncle Jedd detected, with microscopic eye, the marked disapproval of Providence.

If such was the significance of the unheralded shower that drenched Rivermouth's spring bonnets, and bedraggled alike the just and the unjust, it was not so accepted by the congregation of the Old Brick Church.

The Rev. Mr. Dillingham had achieved a signal triumph, and had triumphed in the teeth of very serious obstacles. A small number of the parishioners had been against him from the first, and the death of Parson Hawkins had not only strengthened their opposition, but created a reaction among those who had insisted most strenuously on the removal of the old minister. It so chanced, then, that Mr. Dillingham came to face as critical and unsympathetic a congregation as could well be. Perhaps the only really impartial listeners among his audience were those belonging to other parishes; for it was a noticeable fact that all the other churches in town were nearly empty on this occasion. The Rev. Josiah Jones, who had not spared himself in preparing his sermon for that forenoon, saw with ill-concealed distaste that the larger portion of his flock had strayed into the neighboring pasture.

If Mr. Dillingham had had an intimation of the actual state of things, he would possibly not have been so little self-conscious and so entirely composed as he appeared; but happily he had no suspicion of the unfriendly spirit that animated the majority of his hearers.

With a slight flush on his cheeks, which faded out almost immediately, Mr. Dillingham passed from the small room at the rear of the church, and ascended the pulpit stairs — a slim young man, nearly six feet in height, with gentle blue eyes, and long hair of a dull gold color, which he wore brushed behind his ears. It was not a remarkably strong face, Mr. Dillingham's, but it was not without character. The firmly cut mouth and chin saved it, perhaps, from being effeminate. He was twenty-nine or thirty, but did not look it; his closely shaved face and light complexion gave him quite a youthful air, to one looking at him across the church.

"Why, he ain't nothin' but a boy," said Uncle Jedd to himself, regarding the new minister critically for a moment from the vestibule. "*He* won't do." And the ancient sexton gave a final tug at the bell-rope which he had retained in his hand. While the reverberation of the silvery crash that followed was floating above the house-tops and stealing away to die among the outlying hills, Uncle Jedd softly closed the green-baize doors which opened upon the three aisles.

A contagious ripple and flutter had passed over the congregation when Mr. Dillingham ascended the pulpit steps and seated himself in the antique high-backed chair at the left of the desk. This same flutter and ripple was duplicated as he rose to open the service, which he did by repeating the Lord's Prayer in a clear, melodious voice, making it seem a new thing to some who had only heard it droned before. Quick, subtle glances, indicative of surprise and approval, were shot from pew to pew. The old familiar hymn, too, as he read it, gathered fresh beauty from his lips. A chapter from the Scriptures followed, in which Mr.

Dillingham touched the keynote of his sermon. There was a strange light come into the gentle blue eyes now, and the serene, pale face that had seemed to promise so little was alive with intelligence.

By the time he had reached this portion of the service, the young minister had taken more than half of his listeners captive. The sermon itself completed the victory — Mr. Seth Wiggins and Uncle Jedd alone remaining unconquered, the former having dropped into oblivious slumber after the first hymn, and the latter having retreated into the belfry, where he had sat ruminative on a rafter, communing with the glossy pigeons and ring-doves, until it was time for him to open the doors below.

Mr. Wiggins awoke instinctively, with a jerk, for the benediction, and assumed that half-deprecatory, half-defiant expression which marks the chronic delinquent ; and Uncle Jedd threw open the padded doors just at the critical instant, as if he had been waiting there a century.

As the people filed out of church, both these gentlemen were made aware that the new minister had created a deep impression on the congregation. A drizzling warm rain had begun to fall, as I have said, and groups of elderly ladies and pretty girls, grasping their skirts with despairing clutches, stood about the vestibule waiting for umbrellas to be brought.

"A young man of uncommon talent," Mr. Lathers, the master of the Boys' High School, was heard to remark to Mr. Gargoyle, the retired plumber.

"Oh, uncommon!" responded that gentleman.

"I think he is just perfectly splendid," said Miss Imogen Browne, bringing her creaseless lavender gloves together ecstatically.

"So modest," said Miss Hesba Godfrey.

"And such fine eyes," chimed Miss Amelia, the younger sister.

"How lovely it was in him," remarked Miss Blydenburgh, composedly fastening her bracelet, which had come unlinked, and giving it a little admonitory pat, "to choose for his text the very verse which Parson Hawkins was reading when he died — 'Thou good and faithful servant,' etc., etc."

"And how beautifully he spoke of Parson Hawkins," said young Mrs. Newbury, looking distractingly cool and edible — something like celery — in her widow's weeds. "I was ready to cry."

"*I* did."

"What a spiritual face he has!" observed the elder Miss Trippew, who painted in watercolors; "it reminded me of our Saviour's in the engraving of Leonardo da Vinci's Last Supper."

"And what a delicious voice — like Wendell Phillips's."

"Then such a sermon! It is certainly an improvement on the poor old parson's interminable ninthlies and finallies."

"I wonder if he is married," said Miss Candace Woodman, a compact little person, with almond-shaped brown eyes and glittering yellow ringlets which might have been sent to the Mint and cut up instantly into five-dollar gold-pieces.

Miss Candace's remark cast a strange gloom for a moment over the group in which she stood. Presently the umbrellas appeared; snowy skirts were daintily gathered up; the vestibule was deserted; the voices melted away into the distance. Here and there along the streets, darting to and fro in the rain like swallows, one might have caught scores of such light-winged adjectives as enthusiastic young women let loose when they give expression to their admiration.

"Well, well," muttered Uncle Jedd, turning the key in the ponderous lock of the church-door, "I dunno what th' world is a-comin' ter!"

PRUDENCE PALFREY 149

"And what do you think of Mr. Dillingham, Prue?" asked Mr. Dent, as the hoofs of the horses struck on the slippery planks of the bridge leading from town.

Mr. Dent had not even blinked that day in church. It had been noticed and commented on by the local satirist, that that suspicious smooth place on the wooden pillar intersecting the northwest corner of Mr. Dent's pew was not covered once during the sermon. Mr. Dent himself had observed that "damnéd spot" for the first time with remorse, and had secretly determined to have the interior of the church repainted at his own expense.

"I think," said Prudence, in reply to her guardian's question — "I think he reads well and speaks well."

"Gad, I never heard anybody speak better, except one, and that was Daniel Webster."

"He is very handsome, and seems to be unconscious that he is conscious of it."

"I declare, Prue, you are too deep for me!"

"Is n't he, and with good reason, just a little bit — you know — meekly conceited?"

"Not at all," said Mr. Dent. "I don't know a man with less conceit than Dillingham. He is in earnest. He is going to be very much interested in his work here, and will make his mark. I am only afraid we shall not be able to keep so brilliant a fellow."

"Why not?"

"When he becomes known, some wealthy Boston or New York society will be sure to make him tempting offers."

"But if he is very much interested in his work here, he will not be tempted."

"Perhaps not. But the best of them like fat salaries," said Mr. Dent.

Prudence pictured to herself Parson Wibird deserting the North Parish, or any parish where he thought his duty lay, to accept a call from some richer congregation; but she was not able to draw a distinct picture of it.

"Then I suppose the fatter the salary is the deeper the interest they take in their work?" Prudence remarked.

"Yes," said Mr. Dent shortly.

He felt that he had cast a reflection upon his friend Dillingham; he did not see exactly how, and it annoyed him. The rest of the ride home was in silence. Prudence, too, was not satisfied with herself. In intimating that she thought Mr. Dillingham conceited, she had departed from her usual candor.

Throughout the services his manner had been without a tinge of self-consciousness. She had taken her seat in the pew rather sadly. To see a new minister standing in the place hallowed so many years by the presence of Parson Wibird — it was only a fortnight ago that he stood there, with his placid, venerable face — could but be painful to her. The first few words Mr. Dillingham uttered had grated on her heart; then she had yielded insensibly to the charm which had fallen upon most of the congregation, and found herself listening to him with hushed breath. The strains of the organ seemed to take up the prayer where he had paused; the tones of his voice and the rich swell of the music blended and appeared to have one meaning, like those frescoes in which the same design repeats itself in different tints. She listened and listened, and when Uncle Jedd suddenly threw open the muffled green doors, it was as if a spell had been broken. Oh, glorious gift of speaking golden words with a golden tongue!

A sense of having been disloyal to the memory of the old parson was troubling Prudence when Mr. Dent put his question, and she had not answered him fairly. It was sins like that which Prudence would have had to confess if she had been a Roman Catholic.

She liked Mr. Dillingham more than she had believed it possible to like Parson Wibird's successor; but the limitations of her character would not allow her to acknowledge it upon compulsion. On leaving the church she felt in her heart that she disliked Mr. Dillingham for having made her listen to him; and there shaped itself in Prudence's mind an inexplicable wish — often enough she thought of it afterwards — that he had never come to Rivermouth.

XI

A NEW ENGLAND IDOL

On the following Sunday the Rev. James Dillingham was formally installed pastor of the Old Brick Church. The Rev. Josephus Starleigh delivered the installation sermon (afterwards printed in pamphlet form at the request of the parish), and Mr. Thomas Jefferson Greene, a young poet of local celebrity, composed an original hymn for the occasion.

So the mantle of Parson Wibird Hawkins fell upon the shoulders of the young minister, and the solemn chant ascended, while the great guns were booming down South.

Those were the days — what ages ago they seem! — when the tap of the snare-drum and the shrill treble of the fife startled New England from her dream, and awoke the vengeful echoes which had been slumbering in the mountain fastnesses and among the happy valleys for nearly half a century.

It had long ceased to be at Mr. Dillingham's option to return to South Carolina, and he must have congratulated himself on having found so pleasant a haven as Rivermouth to rest in until the simoom blew over. And certainly Rivermouth congratulated itself on sheltering so brilliant a young divine. I happened to be there at that period, recovering from a protracted illness, and I had the privilege of witnessing a spectacle which is possible only in genteel decayed old towns like that in which the scene of my story lies. To see one or two hundred young New England vestals burning incense and strewing flowers before a slim young gentleman in black is a spectacle worth witnessing once in the course of one's life.

The young man who, putting behind him the less spiritual rewards of other professions, selects the ministry as the field of his labors — drawn to his work by the consciousness that it is there his duty points — is certain to impress us with the purity of his purpose. That he should exert a stronger influence over our minds than a young lawyer does, or a young merchant, or a young man in any respectable walk of life, is easily understood. But a young man, because he buttons the top button of his coat and wears a white necktie, is not necessarily a person of exalted purpose or shining ability. Yet he is apt, without any very searching examination, to be so regarded in some of our provincial towns. I think the straight-cut black coat must possess a subtile magnetism in itself, something analogous to the glamour there is in the uniform of a young naval or army officer. How else shall we explain the admiration which we have many a time seen lavished on very inferior young men?

I am not speaking in this vein of the Rev. James Dillingham. The secret of his popularity was an open secret. It was his manly bearing and handsome face and undeniable eloquence that made him a favorite at once in Rivermouth, and would have commended him anywhere. If Mr. Dillingham turned the heads of all the young women in the parish, he won the hearts of nearly all the elderly people also. I think he would have done this by his amiability and talents, if he had not been rich or young or handsome. If he had been married? Well, I cannot say about that. A young unmarried clergyman, especially if he is rich, is likely to be well thought of in a sequestered valley where there are a surplus of blooming Rachels and a paucity of available Jacobs.

From my point of view, it was something of an ordeal that Mr. Dillingham passed through in those first three months. As much as I admired his sermons, and they were above the average both in style and texture, I admired greatly more the modest good sense which enabled him to keep his bark trim in those pleasant but perilous waters. A vain man would have been wrecked in a week. But the Rev. Mr. Dillingham, as Mr. Ralph Dent had declared, was without conceit of the small kind. The attentions Mr. Dillingham received from all quarters would have gone far to spoil eight men in ten placed in his position. It is so easy to add another story to the high opinion which other persons have of you.

There were evening parties made for Mr. Dillingham at the Blydenburghs', the Goldstones', and the Grimes's; there were picnics up the river, and excursions down the harbor, and innumerable teaings on shore. I do not know if Mr. Dillingham had a very strong sense of humor; but even if he were only mildly humorous, he must have been amused as well as embarrassed by the number of embroidered slippers and ingenious pen-wipers and study-caps and carved paper-cutters that fell to his lot at the fair held about this time for the benefit of the foreign missions. If he had been a centipede he could not have worn out the slippers under four years, wearing them day and night; if he had been a hydra he could not have made head against the study-caps in a lifetime. Briareus would have lacked hands to hold the paper-cutters. The slippers overran Mr. Dillingham's bedroom like the swarms of locusts that settled upon Egypt. The pen-wipers made his study-table look like a bed of variegated dahlias.

There were other expressions of regard, less material and tangible than these, to be sure, but which must have been infinitely harder to dispose of. There were sudden droopings of eyelashes, black or golden, when he spoke; furtive glances of shyness or reverence; half-parted lips, indicating that breathless interest which is the very cream of compliment, and flies to the head like wine.

Mr. Dillingham moved gracefully and serenely among the shoals and quicksands; he listened to the songs of the sirens, and passed on. He did not, however, accept the flattery as if it were only his due; he accepted it modestly, and was simply natural, and candid, and good-natured, like a man who finds himself among friends. "I see how it is," he once remarked to Mr. Dent, "I am standing in the sunshine created by my predecessor." It was no glory of his own; he was fortunate in falling among a people who took kindly to their minister.

If Mr. Dillingham had been blind, he might

have seen that he could have his choice of Rivermouth's belles; and he was far from sightless. He read women and men very well in his quiet fashion. Clearly, he was in no haste to be fettered. What a crowd of keen, fair slave-merchants would have flocked down to the market-place, if this slender, blond prince from Southland had been chained by the ankle to one of the stalls, to be knocked down by Mr. Wiggins to the highest bidder!

Miss Veronica Blydenburgh, who passed her winters in New York and Baltimore, and had flirted in a high-spirited way with various professions, became suddenly pensive. Hesba Godfrey candidly owned that she had fallen in love with Mr. Dillingham before he got halfway up the pulpit stairs the first Sunday, but that Fred Shelborne refused to release her, and she supposed she should be obliged to marry Fred — just to keep him quiet. Young Mrs. Newbury in her widow's weeds, like a diamond set in jet, seemed to grow lovelier day by day. In my own mind I put the widow down as dangerous. Not that I had any reason for so doing. Mr. Dillingham smiled upon her with precisely the same smile he gave to the Widow Mugridge. There was not a shade of difference perceptible between his manner to the elder Miss Trippew, a remarkably plain lamb, and his manner to Miss Veronica of the golden fleece. I said it before, and I say again, I admired the way he carried himself through all this.

When Mr. Dillingham, the morning following his initial sermon, signified to the deacons his acceptance of the pastorate of the Old Brick Church, a knotty question arose as to the residence of the new minister. There was no parsonage attached to the church; the cottage which Parson Hawkins had occupied so many years did not belong to the society; besides, if there had been a parsonage, Mr. Dillingham had no family, and the absurdity of his going to housekeeping without a family was obvious. The three or four private boarding-places suggested to him failed to meet his views. Deacon Twombly, who saw the advantage of having a lucrative boarder, hinted at his first floor as furnishing desirable accommodation; but the ewe-lamb was brought up as an objection.

Mr. Dillingham, who was staying at the Old Bell Tavern, the only hotel in town — having declined Mr. Dent's offer of hospitality — cut the Gordian knot by deciding to remain where he was.

This gave a sensible shock to some of the congregation, for it seemed scarcely proper for the pastor of the Old Brick Church to live at a hotel. Deacon Wendell adroitly intimated as much to Mr. Dillingham, who replied that he did not see why it was proper for him to remain six days at the hotel, as he had done, if it was improper for him to remain there six months, or six years. Propriety was not a question of time. The house was quiet, his rooms commodious and comfortable, and he did not see how he could do better. He invited Deacon Wendell to dinner, and no further objections were heard of.

In the first bloom of his popularity Mr. Dillingham could have done pretty much as he pleased, and he did.

Among other innovations, he brought sunshine into the Old Brick Church. Parson Hawkins had been a good man, a saint, indeed; but his saintliness had been of the sombre sort; listening to some of his doctrinal sermons, one might have applied to him that epigram of Landor's —

> "'Fear God!' says Percival; and when you hear
> Tones so lugubrious, you perforce must fear:
> If in such awful accents he should say,
> 'Fear lovely Innocence!' you 'd run away!"

That early Puritan taint which sometimes appeared in Parson Hawkins's theology, but never in his daily life, was an alien thing to

Mr. Dillingham in or out of the pulpit. The spirit of his teaching was eminently a cheerful spirit.

There was a new order of things in the North Parish. The late parson had stood a great deal of browbeating first and last. A conservative man, leaning perhaps a little too heavily on the pillars of the church, he had ever consulted the inclination of the deacons. They had an independent minister now ; a parson who settled questions for himself, and did not embarrass his mind by loading it with outside opinions. There was a spice of novelty in this surprisingly agreeable to the palate of a community long accustomed to domineer over its pastor. How long will it last ? I used to wonder. I had seen so many idols set up reverently, and bowled over ruthlessly, that I was slightly sceptical as to the duration of Mr. Dillingham's popularity. If the townsfolk were image-worshippers, they were iconoclasts also, when the mood was on them. But Mr. Dillingham's popularity did not wane during my three months' stay in Rivermouth ; it went on steadily increasing. The war-fever was at its height in those months ; and the loyalty of Mr. Dillingham, a Southerner, stood out in striking contrast with the mild patriotism of several of our native-born statesmen. When his first quarter's salary fell due, Mr. Dillingham set the seal to public favor by turning over the amount to the fund for the Soldiers' Hospital. Uncle Jedd himself, one of the last in the parish that held out against the new minister, was obliged to admit that this was very handsome in the young man.

Mr. Dillingham had not been three weeks in Rivermouth before he knew all the queer old men and women in the place, and stood in their good graces. Even the one habitual drunkard, when he was not hiding the rosy light of his countenance at the Town-Farm, would touch his battered hat convulsively, meeting the young parson on the street.

Mr. Dillingham was gifted in a high degree with the genius for knowing people, and displayed consummate tact in his dealings with the poor of the parish. When he made the Widow Pepperell and the Clemmer boys his pensioners, he did it so delicately that the obligation seemed on his side. "The parson's smile," said Sandy Marden, "jest doubles what he gives a feller." Jeremiah Bowditch, the unfortunate inebriate mentioned — a shy, morbid man, and as sensitive as an exposed nerve — was not afraid to apply to the parson for a dollar, having discovered that the coin would not be dropped upon him from such a moral height as to knock the breath out of his body and wound all his finer feelings.

"What I like in Dillingham," said the Hon. Sam Knubley, democratic member of the General Court, "is that there is n't any 'first-family' nonsense about him. You can see with half an eye that he belongs to the Southern aristocracy, but he is n't eternally shinning up his genealogical tree. There's old Blydenburgh, who is always perching himself on the upper branches and hurling down the cocoa-nuts of his ancestors at common folks."

It is not to be supposed that the Hon. Sam Knubley himself would have objected to a few brilliant ancestors. To have the right to fall in at the end of a long queue of men and women distinguished in their day and generation, is a privilege which none but a simpleton would undervalue. It is a privilege, however, which often has its drawbacks. Much is expected of a man whose progenitors have been central figures. To inherit the great name without the great gifts is a piece of ironical good fortune. When one's ancestors have been everything, and one's self is nothing, it is perhaps just as well not to demand from the world the same degree of consideration that was given voluntarily to one's predecessors. I have encountered two or three young gentlemen in the capital of the Commonwealth of Massachusetts who seemed to have the idea that *they* were killed at the battle of Bunker Hill. It was possibly this sort of assumption that displeased the Hon. Sam Knubley; if so, the Hon. Sam Knubley was quite right in the matter.

Mr. Dent witnessed with pride the success of his young friend; and Prudence, who, by the way, had naturally seen a great deal of Mr. Dillingham meanwhile, began to take herself to task for her cold demeanor towards him.

If the truth must be told, she had been far from cordial to Mr. Dillingham. Now, it is as mortifying to have one's lack of cordiality unnoticed as it is to have one's warmth overlooked. Mr. Dillingham had apparently not observed that Miss Palfrey had treated him with haughtiness. If she had been the Widow Mugridge, he could not have smiled upon her more benignly, or listened to her more attentively, when she was pleased to address him. The offence to her self-love was so subtile that Prudence was never able to account for the restless and half-provoked mood which, up to this time, had always possessed her in his presence.

"The fact is," Prudence soliloquized one

evening when the young clergyman had taken tea at Willowbrook, " I have an unamiable disposition; Uncle Ralph has spoiled me by humoring me. I must discipline myself, and I'll begin by treating Mr. Dillingham with a little politeness, if his royal highness will allow it. I always feel as if he stepped down from a throne to converse with me. In spite of his smile and deference, when one is speaking, there's something depressing and condescending in his air. If King Cophetua was the least like that, I wonder the beggar maid had anything to do with him."

It was, by the way, Miss Veronica Blydenburgh who had christened him King Cophetua.

XII

PRUE!

Though the Rev. Mr. Dillingham had too much diplomacy to stroke one lamb on the head more tenderly than another, and so throw the whole flock into confusion, he made no secret of his preference for Mr. Dent.

Mr. Dillingham passed most of his leisure hours at Willowbrook. Since his installation, he had taken tea there every Sunday evening. When Mr. Dent went to town, which was three or four times a week, he always dropped into his friend's study, and frequently Mr. Dillingham rode home with him and remained to dinner. There was a well-stocked fish-pond a few miles beyond Willowbrook; both gentlemen were expert anglers, and they spent their mornings together in the season. Then there were horseback rides, in which Prudence occasionally joined. Mr. Dillingham had purchased a fine animal, which he rode admirably.

"We all ride in the South," he said to Miss Palfrey. "The people in the town stare at me as if I were a part of a circus caravan, but I trust they will get accustomed to the sight. A saddle-horse is a necessity to me; I have had one since I was six years old. To drive around in a gig with side-lanterns, like great goggles, as that good soul Dr. Tredick does, would kill me. I should never get out alive so far as Willowbrook, Miss Palfrey. I'd much prefer being brought here in Mr. Plunket's hand-cart."

Plunket was a harmless, half-witted old fellow about town who picked up a living by carrying packages in a small hand-cart as aged and shattered as himself. He had not escaped Mr. Dillingham, whose eye for every sort of eccentric character was, as I have said, exceptionally keen.

The friendship between Mr. Dillingham and Mr. Dent deepened as the weeks passed, and the latter gentleman experienced something like a sinking at heart whenever his thought recurred to the possibility that his young friend might be tempted some time or other to desert Rivermouth for a more extended field of operation.

"I wish to heaven, Dillingham," exclaimed Mr. Dent one evening at the tea-table, "that you would give up your apartments in town, and come out here with us. There's a cosey room leading from the south chamber that would make a capital study for you."

"I am afraid I should find it too pleasant," returned Mr. Dillingham, "and fall into a habit of not working. Besides, my parish calls? I am very sensible of your kindness, my friend; but, really, I think I am better off in my present quarters. You see, two sermons a week keep me pretty busy. Then I am not a lark as regards early rising. I should be a dreadful infliction in a private house. All Miss Palfrey's methodical domestic laws would be overthrown at once."

"I'd like to be an eyewitness to that," Mr. Dent said, laughing; "her law is as the law of the Medes and Persians, which altereth not. Prue is a regular martinet in the commissary department."

"I really am," spoke Prudence for herself. "If one is not down in time, one gets a cold breakfast."

"There, you see," said Mr. Dillingham. "Now there are two things I never can do; I cannot endure a cold breakfast, and I never can get down early to a warm one."

In spite of this obstacle, however, Mr. Dillingham often occupied that spare room with the southern exposure, which Mr. Dent had mentioned, sometimes spending several days in succession with his Willowbrook friends. Then they met him continually in society in town, and in point of fact saw as much of him as if he had accepted Mr. Dent's proposition.

This intimacy could not fail to give rise to remarks. It was soon whispered, and not too softly, that the young minister was paying attentions to Mr. Dent's ward. Now, though Prudence's coldness had moderated somewhat, and she no longer had to make exertions to be polite to Mr. Dillingham, Mr. Dillingham had not in the least changed his manner to her. She was aware, and the reflection sometimes piqued her, that she was no better acquainted with him after months of intercourse than she was on the day she first saw him. Perhaps it was her own fault they were not warmer friends in the beginning; but it was not her fault now. She had learned to respect his character, to admire his intellect, and to derive a quiet pleasure from his presence; but she had evidently not taught him to like her more than he had liked her at the start. This was not flattering under the circumstances. The inference was, Mr. Dillingham disliked her, and tolerated her only on account of his friendship for Mr. Dent.

Prudence secretly resented this, and formed a misty idea that it would be an agreeable thing to have him fall slightly in love with her, not seriously in love, but just enough to enable her to teach him a lesson. This idea, in no respect a commendable one, took a more definite shape, and became almost a wish subsequently. Nice young women are not to be treated cavalierly with impunity.

It was rumored at first that Mr. Dillingham was very much interested in Miss Palfrey; that was sufficiently annoying; but later on, rumor changed its tactics, and reported that Miss Palfrey was very much interested in Mr. Dillingham. Gossip, like Providence, is inscrutable in its ways; it has its laws, we may suppose, clearly defined, if one could get at them; but they are not to be reached by inductive reasoning, and it must remain a mystery how it came to be believed in Rivermouth that Prudence was very unhappy in consequence of her unreturned love for Mr. Dillingham.

To say that she did not hear of this exasperating story as soon as it was born, would be to say that Prudence had no intimate female friend, and there was Miss Veronica Blydenburgh.

"And there is n't the least shadow of truth in it, Prue?" said Veronica.

"Not the faintest. How absurd! I don't

care that for him," said Prudence, measuring off an infinitesimal portion of her little finger's tip, "nor he for me. He and Uncle Ralph talk fish-hooks and theology and war, and I don't believe Mr. Dillingham has noticed whether I am sixteen or sixty."

"Dear me," said Veronica thoughtfully.

"Mortifying, is n't it?"

"To be sure it is."

"I like him, of course," continued Prudence; "he is extremely agreeable, and all that. If there was, or could be, anything more, I should be the first to tell you."

"Dear me," repeated Veronica. "And it came so straight — from the Goldstones, you know." And Veronica, who had put her interrogation rather solemnly, became unnecessarily merry over the absurdity of the thing.

"The Goldstones?" said Prue. "I am very grateful to them!"

After they had parted, Prudence thought of the abrupt change of mood in her friend, and it brought her to a full stop in the middle of the bridge, for Prudence was walking in from Rivermouth. Then she recalled a trivial incident that had taken place a few nights before in town, at a party at the Blydenburghs'. It had made no impression on her at the time, but now she recalled it. Veronica had missed her bracelet late in the evening, a valuable bracelet, a large opal with diamonds. She had been in the garden; she had danced in the parlors; and had gone twice to the supper-room. The bracelet was not to be found in the house, and Veronica with several of the guests, among others Prudence and Mr. Dillingham, went into the garden to search for it in a certain arbor where ices had been served. There were a score or two of Chinese lanterns hung about the trellis-work, and the place was as light as day. In bending over the sward Mr. Dillingham had inadvertently brushed against Veronica's shoulder — that snowy shoulder which had such an innocent arch way of shrinking from the corsage — and Veronica had started back with a pretty cry, blushing absurdly. Mr. Dillingham had been disconcerted for an instant, then he had bowed in a formal way to Veronica.

This little scene came up before Prudence's eyes again, and she walked on in a reverie.

"It would be a very good match, though," said Prudence, thinking aloud.

The piece of gossip which Miss Blydenburgh had unfolded to her friend vexed that young lady exceedingly. The other rumor, placing Mr. Dillingham at her feet, had vexed her too; but that could have been borne. It sank into insignificance beside this new version, in which she was made to play the heroine with dishevelled hair and unrequited affections — a rôle to which she was not kindly disposed; for Prudence was as proud as Mrs. Lucifer, if I may make the comparison without assuming the responsibility of creating the personage.

Prudence's prompt impulse was to fall back on her former frosty manner towards Mr. Dillingham; but that was hardly practicable now; besides, the Rivermouth censors would be sure to misconstrue her indifference and attribute it to wounded vanity.

Her wisest course was to treat Mr. Dillingham naturally, and let the shameless scandal die of its own inanity. He would never hear the silly report; there was no one who would venture to touch on so delicate a matter with him. Even the Widow Mugridge, who was capable of almost anything in that line, might be pictured as shrinking before such an attempt; for though Mr. Dillingham was as generally affable and approachable as the sunshine, his familiarity did not breed contempt. In the sea of adulation that dimpled around him, there was a gentle under-tow of wholesome respect. The young clergyman's independence and sharpness, when called for, were quite well understood in the parish. He had wit, but no humor; and the difference between wit and humor, it seems to me, is just the difference between an open and a shut penknife. So there was no chance of anybody coming to him with tittle-tattle, especially about Miss Palfrey.

Having settled this in her mind, Prudence calmed; but the gossip still rankled in her bosom, and she felt it would be a most satisfying vindication and triumph if Mr. Dillingham would only fall in love with her mildly, and afford her the opportunity of proving that she did not care for him, in that way.

In other ways she cared for him greatly. Indeed, she had a strong desire for his friendship. Every one had always liked her; she had never been courteously snubbed before, or snubbed at all, and had no taste for it. The hurt went deeper than her vanity. It was a shocking novelty to encounter a person — a person whom she esteemed, too — whose whole demeanor said to her as plainly as words, but politely, of course: "Miss Palfrey, when you laugh, and say sharp things to me, I smile upon you; when you are demure and repentant and inclined to be friendly, I smile upon you all the same; for, really, I do not care whether you are amiable or unamiable. It is a matter that concerns you, and you alone."

If Mr. Dillingham had studied Prudence from her infancy, and had wished to win her regard, he could not have proceeded more judiciously. It is true, John Dent did not win her by this method; but she was younger then, and may be off her guard. Perhaps if John Dent had had it to do over again, he might not have found it so easy. What is efficacious at seventeen or eighteen is by no means certain of success at twenty-one.

Prudence did not think often of John Dent at this epoch. The phantom that had haunted her so long had somehow withdrawn itself. For four or five months now she had breathed with a conscious sense of freedom from the past. Mr. Dent's letters to Montana and California had brought no response, and the subject of the will was one that could well lie in abeyance. Nothing could be done about it, and it was not agreeable to talk or think about.

Mr. Dent observed with pleasure Prudence's growing appreciation of Mr. Dillingham, and had some views which he cautiously kept to himself. Nothing would have delighted him more than to see Prue well married now, however much the idea of losing her had distracted him two or three years before; but he was not going to interfere. He had once come near making her very unhappy, and had learned to distrust his own sagacity in matters of the heart. He purposed in the present case to let things take their own course.

Things were taking their course, perhaps a little lazily, but on the whole to his satisfaction. Prudence was never so lovely or sweet-tempered, and Mr. Dent wondered time and again that Dillingham did not see more clearly than he seemed to see that Prudence was a very charming young person. Mr. Dillingham held the stirrup for her to mount Jenny, he folded her shawl neatly under the carriage-seat, and was remiss in none of those attentions which a well-bred man pays to a lady, young or old; but in everything he did or said there was an air of having been introduced to Miss Palfrey yesterday. To be sure, he had once or twice addressed her as "Miss Prudence," instead of Miss Palfrey, striking her speechless with astonishment; but then he had corrected himself in the same breath.

"Why in the deuce does n't he call her Prue, like everybody else?" muttered Mr. Dent. "He has known her five months intimately, and Jack called her Prue after fifteen minutes' acquaintance. But that was Jack all over."

The autumn of this year was unprecedentedly lovely — it was one prolonged Indian summer — and horseback rides early in the morning were the chief diversion at Willowbrook, where Mr. Dillingham frequently remained overnight to accompany Mr. Dent and his ward. If Mr. Dillingham had a constitutional objection to breakfasting with the larks, he had none whatever to rising at five o'clock to take a four-mile gallop along the Rivermouth lanes, now wonderful with their brilliant foliage. Prudence was an excellent horse-woman, and never lagged behind her comrades.

> " As she fled fast through sun and shade
> The happy winds upon her played,
> Blowing the ringlet from the braid."

Mr. Dillingham must have been a stupid fellow if he did not notice how this autumnal weather heightened Prue's beauty. She had caught a trick of color from nature, and made the rosy maple-leaves by the roadside seem tame in tint compared with her rich lips and cheeks.

On one of these excursions Mr. Dent was unlucky enough to sprain his ankle, and the rides came to an end, at least Mr. Dent's did.

Mr. Dillingham, who came often now to read and chat with his friend, rode alone several mornings, and then, rather to the surprise of Prudence, invited her to bear him company.

"Would it be proper for me to go, uncle?"

asked Prudence, standing with drooped eyelids by Mr. Dent's lounge.

"Would it be proper!" he echoed. "Why, the female population of Rivermouth would turn out in a body, and Dillingham would certainly meet the fate of old Floyd Ireson, who, as you remember, was 'tarred and feathered and carried in a cart by the women of Marblehead'!"

"Very well, then," cried Prue gayly, "I'll ride Kate instead of Jenny. Jenny pokes along so, and Mr. Dillingham likes a rapid pace."

"'Pokes along so!' what a phrase from a young lady's lips!" said Mr. Dent critically.

"I said polks," cried Prue shamelessly.

Mr. Dillingham unbent a little that morning. Being in some sense a host, he was constrained to look after the entertainment of his guest and render himself agreeable. The ride was without incident, save its uninterrupted pleasantness, and Prudence returned with her cheeks in bloom and her gray eyes with the daybreak in them.

Three or four days afterwards the young minister rode up to the gate just before sundown, and asked if Miss Palfrey would repeat her gallop. He had discovered a road leading to some old earthworks overlooking the harbor, where the sunset was a thing to see. Kate was saddled, and the two young folks went off in a cloud of dust, Mr. Dent leaning on a cane at the drawing-room window and smiling on them like an amiable Fate.

Mr. Dent's sprained ankle was a phenomenal case, and I am strongly tempted to prepare an elaborate paper on the subject for the pages of the Boston Medical and Surgical Journal. At the time of the accident — he turned his foot in the stirrup while dismounting — it was thought serious enough to merit Dr. Tredick's attention, who relieved Prudence's solicitude by treating the injury lightly. But the weakened limb did not recover its strength, even after a course of arnica bandages that ought to have caused a new leg to grow, or at least to have mended the old one though it had been fractured in twenty places.

The ankle did not get well, and science in the person of Dr. Tredick was at a loss to explain why, and more especially to explain why it should be most troublesome in the afternoons. Mr. Dent was able in the morning to walk on the piazza or go about the house without excessive inconvenience; but towards three or four o'clock, at which hour Mr. Dillingham generally appeared to inquire after the invalid, Mr. Dent found it necessary to take to the lounge in the parlor, or to sit with his foot supported by another chair.

"Don't mind me, Dillingham," Mr. Dent said one day, with touching cheerfulness. "I shall be all right after a while. I miss our rides confoundedly, and I know you detest riding alone. However, there's Prue; she's better than nobody."

"Oh, you flatter me!" says Prue.

"I fear I have already drawn heavily on Miss Prudence's complaisance," replied Mr. Dillingham. He did not correct himself this time. But Prudence was passionately fond of riding, and to ride with Mr. Dillingham was like waltzing with a good partner. She did not require other incitive. So it came about, owing to Mr. Dent's slow recovery, that she often accompanied the young minister alone, not caring greatly now what people said. She was doing nothing wrong, and the innocent enjoyment was an offset to any malicious criticism.

Mr. Dillingham had thawed perceptibly, and in a stately style was very gracious to her. Prudence's passing desire to have him love her a little had evaporated; she was content with his friendship. The severest precision could have discovered nothing to cavil at in Prudence's conduct. As in the old time she had not flirted with John Dent, so in the new she did not flirt with Mr. Dillingham. She made no eyes at him, as Mr. Dent would have stated it, and would have stated it regretfully.

There was not much conversation during these horseback excursions, which usually had the fort for destination; a swift gallop through the bracing autumn air, a halt in the lonely redoubt to breathe the horses and see the sunset, and a dashing gait homeward, being the ends in view.

It was a charming landscape which unrolled itself, like a colored map, at the foot of the precipitous hill crowned by the deserted earthworks. First came a series of cultivated fields, orchards, and gardens, nestled among which were red-roofed barns and comfortable white farm-houses, with striped chimneys, peering through the leafless tree-tops. Then came the river spanned by a many-arched bridge, linking the picturesque town with the open country. Here and there along the wharves the slender masts of fishing-smacks shot up sharply. The clusters of round islands in the harbor were like emeralds set in turquois, for the water at this point, at certain seasons, is of a singularly opaque blue. Beyond the town lay the bright salt marshes softly folded in an azure arm of the sea. All this, in the glow of the declining sun, was fair to look upon.

One November afternoon, in the middle of the month, Prudence and Mr. Dillingham drew rein within the parade-ground of the old fortification just as the sun was sinking. The embrasure at which they halted formed the frame of a fairy picture in which sea and sky and meadow were taking a hundred opaline tints from the reflection of the sunset. While the horses stood champing the bits, and panting, the two riders let the reins slip idly from their fingers, and sat watching the scene in silence.

In a few minutes the vivid colors faded out of the sky, save at the horizon, where a strip of angry scarlet still lingered, leaving the landscape of a soft pearly gray. By and by the strip of scarlet melted into cinnabar, then into faint gold, then into silver, then into indistinguishable ashes-of-roses like the rest, and the early twilight stretched across land and sea.

"It is like a dream, is n't it?" murmured Prue to herself, for at the instant she had forgotten the presence of her companion.

Mr. Dillingham leaned forward without speaking, and laid his hand lightly on Prudence's, which rested ungloved on the black mane of the mare.

The girl lifted her eyes with a swift movement to the face of the young minister, and then very slowly withdrew her hand.

"Prue!" said Mr. Dillingham softly.

XIII

JONAH

Mr. Joseph Twombly was sitting on a high stool at a desk in the counting-room of Messrs. Rawlings & Sons, the Chicago bankers. It was after bank hours, and the office was deserted. The gray-haired head bookkeeper, and the spruce young clerks who occupied the adjoining desks, had been gone an hour or more. The monotonous ticking of the chronometer, pinioned against the wall above the massive iron safe, was the only sound that broke the quiet of the room, except when Twombly made an impatient movement with one of his feet on the attenuated rungs of the stool, or drummed abstractedly with his fingers on the edge of the desk.

An open letter lay before him, and beside it an envelope bearing a Shasta postmark and addressed to Joseph Twombly at Rivermouth. This letter had just come to him enclosed in one of the deacon's, and was to this effect —

SHASTA, CAL., October 31, 186–.

MY DEAR JOE: You will probably be surprised to receive a letter from me after all these months of silence — or, rather, years, for it is nearly three years, is n't it, since we parted? I have been in no mood or condition to write before, and I write now only because I may not have another chance to relieve you of any uncertainty you may feel on my account. I have thought it my duty to do this since I came to the resolve, within a few days, to give up my hopeless pursuits here and go into the army. If you do not hear from me or of me in the course of four or six months, you will know that my bad luck, which began in Montana, has culminated somewhere in the South. Then you can show this to my Uncle Dent, or even before, if you wish; I leave it to your discretion. Perhaps I shall do something in the war; who knows? It is time for me to do something. I am a failure up to date. I 'm not sure I am a brave man, but I have that disregard for life which well fits me to lead forlorn hopes — and I 've led many a forlorn hope these past three years, Joe.

Ever since the day we said good-by at Red Rock, I have been on the go. I have not stayed more than a month in any one spot, except this last half year at a ranch in the neighborhood of Shasta, where I went into the stock-raising business with another man (who did n't know I was the spirit of Jonah revisiting the earth), and would have made my fortune if the cattle disease had not got into the herd just as we were on the point of selling out at great profit. I was not aware that I had the cattle disease myself, but I fancy I must have given it to the herd.

What had I been doing all the rest of the time? — for it took me only six months to ruin my friend the stock-raiser. I had been searching for George Nevins, Joe Twombly!

What a story I could tell you, if I had the heart and the patience to go over it all again! How I first heard of him in California, where I tracked him from place to place, sometimes only an hour or so behind him; once I entered a mining-camp just as he went out the other side, confound his cleverness! — how I followed him to Texas, and thence to Montana again, and from there to Mexico, where I lost trace of him; what I suffered mentally and physically in those mad hunts would not be believed if I could write it out — how I worked my way from town to town, and from camp to camp, only halting here and there to earn a few dollars to help me on. Hunger, thirst, cold, and heat, I have known them all, Joe, as few men have known them. Shall I tell you — and that is the strangest thing! — what took the life out of me more than the poverty and the treachery and the rest? It was the conviction that that man, though I could not put my hand on *him*, had his eye on *me* all the while — the certainty that I never went to sleep without his knowing where I lay down, that I never got up but he was advised of my next move, that I was under his espionage day and night.

I think my steps were dogged from the time I first left Montana, though I had no suspicion of it until long after. The suspicion fired me and gave me strength in the beginning, and then it paralyzed me, when I saw how easily he eluded my pursuit, and how defenceless I was. I could trust nobody. The fellow sleeping at my side by the camp-fire might be Nevins's spy. Every stranger that looked at me any way curiously sent a chill to my heart. Whether there were three men or a hundred employed to watch me, I cannot tell; but at every point there was some one to mislead me or balk my plan. The wilds of Montana seemed to be policed by this terrible man. Why did n't he kill me, and have done with it? I don't know. My life was in his hands, and is to-day. The sense of being surrounded and dogged and snared grew insupportable at last. Can you understand how maddening it was? I gave up the hope of meeting Nevins face to face, and only longed to hide myself somewhere out of his sight.

About six months ago I fell in with a man at Shasta, one Thompson, who owned a ranch twenty miles back in the country; he wanted help in managing his herds, and offered me a share in the stock. This business has just turned out disastrously, as I have said. Everything I touch turns worthless. It was a sorry day for you, poor Joe, when you joined fortune with me. I could sink a cork ship. I am Jonah without Jonah's whale. If ever I am thrown overboard, I shall be drowned, mark that.

I had to leave the ranch, and left it two days ago. The moment I put foot in Shasta I felt I was again under the eye of Nevins's invisible police. I am not sure I shall escape them by going into the army. I am not sure, on patriotic grounds, that I *ought* to go into the army. My luck is enough to bring on a national defeat.

In all these thirty-six months, Joe, I had not heard a word from Rivermouth — until last night. I suppose you must have written to me; if you have, your letters missed fire. No one else, I imagine, has been much troubled about my fate. My dear old friend, Parson Wibird, is dead, and Miss Palfrey is going to marry his successor. So runs the world away! These two items of news gave a hard tug at my heart-strings. I got the intelligence in the oddest way. Last night, sitting on the porch of the hotel, I overheard a stranger talking about Rivermouth. You may fancy I pricked up my ears at the word, and invented occasion to speak with the man. He did not belong to the town, but he appeared to have come from there lately, and I gathered from him all I wanted to know — and more! O Joe! there are things in the world that cut one up more cruelly than hunger and cold. But I can't write of this. I did not mean to write so long a letter; I meant only to let you know I was alive. Indeed, I am in frightfully good health. If I had been rich and happy, I might have been dead these two years. "There's nae luck aboot the house!"

I'm not breathing a word of reproach against anybody, you understand. I haven't the right. I have made my own bed, and if I don't lie in it comfortably, there's no one to blame except myself. I see my mistake. I ought to have stayed at Red Rock, and gone to work again, like a man. But it's too late now.

Good-by, my dear Joe. I hope you are prospering, you and your tribe. There must be a lot of you by this time! You continue, I suppose, to have an annual brother or sister? I trust Uncle Dent is well also. He is a fine old fellow, and I've regretted a thousand times that I quarrelled with him. But he *did* brush my hair the wrong way. I start from here to-morrow for the East. I have not decided yet whether to join the army in the North or in the West; but wherever I go, I am, my dear boy,
Your faithful and unfortunate friend,
JOHN DENT.

Mr. Joseph Twombly read the eight pages through twice very carefully, interrupting himself from time to time to give vent to an exclamation of surprise or pity or disapproval or indignation, as the mood moved him.

"Poor Jack!" said Twombly. "He *is* a kind of Jonah, sure enough, and I don't believe the healthiest whale in the world could keep him on its stomach for five minutes. What a foolish fellow to throw himself away in that fashion! Why in thunder didn't he tell me where to write him? October 31. That's more than a month ago. The Lord only knows what may have happened since then."

Twombly sat pondering for some time with

his elbows on the desk; then he folded up the letter, and placed it in a fresh envelope, which he directed in a large, round, innocent hand to " Ralph Dent, Esq., Rivermouth, N. H."

XIV

KING COPHETUA AND THE BEGGAR MAID

Mr. Dent had watched the increasing intimacy between Prudence and the young minister with much peculiar, secret satisfaction, as the reader has been informed; and that afternoon, while she and Mr. Dillingham were gazing at the sunset through the embrasure of the fort, Mr. Dent, in spite of the pain in his ankle, of which he had complained earlier in the day, was walking briskly up and down the library, building castles for the young pair.

When a man has reached the age of Mr. Dent, and is too rheumatic himself to occupy castles in the air, he indulges in this kind of architecture for the benefit of others, that is, if he has a generous nature, and Mr. Dent had a very generous nature. To see Prue well settled in life, and to have two or three of Prue's children playing around the armchair of his old age, was his only dream now. So, in constructing his castles, he added to each a wing for a nursery on a scale more extensive, perhaps, than would have been approved by either of the prospective tenants, if the architect had submitted his plans to them.

Mr. Dent had never asked himself — and possibly the question would have posed him — why he was so willing now for Prudence to marry, when the thought of her marrying had appeared so terrible to him in connection with his nephew. It was John Dent's misfortune, perhaps, that he was the first to stir Mr. Dent's parental jealousy; may be Mr. Dillingham would have fared no better if he had come first. At all events, he had come second, and Mr. Dent was far from raising objections.

He was in the sunniest of humors, this afternoon, contemplating Prue's possible happiness and his own patriarchal comfort in it, when Fanny brought in the evening papers, and with them the letter which Mr. Joseph Twombly had considerately mailed to Mr. Dent a few days before.

He tore open the envelope carelessly, recognizing Twombly's handwriting, but the sight of John Dent's penmanship gave him a turn. He ran over the pages hurriedly, and with various conflicting emotions, among which a sympathy for Jack's past and present sufferings was not, it is to be feared, so pronounced as Twombly's had been.

It was unquestionably a relief to know that Jack was alive and in good health; but it was a little unfortunate to have the letter come just then, when everything was going on so smoothly. The reflection that Jack might take it into his head to return to Rivermouth and insist on marrying Prue was not agreeable to Mr. Dent. He had assented to this at one time; he had overlooked his nephew's poverty, but since then John Dent had not behaved handsomely to Prue.

Whatever Prudence's feelings were, this letter could but disturb her. It would set her to thinking of the past, and that was not desirable. But why show her the letter, at present? — he would have to show it to her if he spoke of it; why not wait until he heard again from Jack, whose plans were still with loose ends? He could not be put into possession of the Hawkins property or even informed that he was to inherit it, for the year specified in the will lacked several months of expiration. Moreover, the letter was one that for several reasons could not well be shown to Prudence; it spoke of her marriage as a foregone conclusion — the very way to unsettle everything; and then what business had Jack to go and say there were things in the world that cut one up more cruelly than hunger and cold? What an intemperate kind of phraseology that was!

These reflections were struggling through Mr. Dent's mind when he heard the clatter of hoofs at the gate. He crumpled the letter in his hand, and thrusting it into his pocket, hastened out to the front door. In the middle of the hall he recollected what a bad state his ankle was in, and limped the rest of the way.

"Won't you stop to tea, Dillingham?" he cried, as he saw the young clergyman with one foot in the stirrup, Mr. Dillingham having dismounted to assist Prudence from the saddle.

"Thanks, my friend; but to-night, you know, is the night I am obliged to prepare my sermon."

With which words Mr. Dillingham touched his hat to Miss Palfrey, waved his hand smilingly to Mr. Dent, and rode away.

As Prudence came up the gravelled path, with the trail of her riding-habit thrown over her arm, showing two neat bronze boots, she was too much engaged with her own thoughts to notice Mr. Dent closely; at another time she would have seen that something had disturbed him. Mr. Dent was sharper sighted, and he saw that Prudence was laboring under unusual excitement. Had Dillingham spoken at last, and if so, how had Prue taken it? He did not dare to conjecture, for he felt it would be a bitter disappointment to him if she had refused Dillingham.

"At any rate," Mr. Dent said to himself, "Jack's letter is not the thing for popular reading just now."

After tea Prudence told her guardian what had passed between her and Mr. Dillingham. He had asked her to be his wife, but so abruptly and unexpectedly, that he had startled her more than she liked. He had, without any warning, leaned forward and taken her hand while they were looking at the sunset in the bastion of the ruined fort; then he had stepped down from his horse, much as King Cophetua must have stepped down from the throne, and stood at her stirrup-side.

Prudence felt it would be dreadfully sentimental to repeat what Mr. Dillingham had said to her, so she did not repeat his words, but gave Mr. Dent the substance of them. The young man perceived that the suddenness of his action had displeased Prudence, and begged to be forgiven for that, and for the abruptness of his words, if they seemed abrupt to her; they did not seem so to him, for he had carried her presence in his thought from the hour he first saw her. If during the past months he had concealed his feelings in regard to her, it was because he knew his own unworthiness, and did not dare to hope for so great happiness as her love would be to him. He had betrayed his secret involuntarily; the hour, the place, and her nearness must plead for him.

"He really turned it very neatly," said Prue, trying to brush off the bloom of romance which she was conscious overspread her story, though she had endeavored to tell it in as prosaic a manner as possible.

"He's a noble fellow," exclaimed Mr. Dent warmly, "and is worthy of any woman — the best of women, and that's you."

"He is noble," said Prudence meditatively; "and as he stood there, looking up at me, I think I more than half loved him."

"And you told him so!" cried Mr. Dent.

"No, I did not," said Prudence, with a perplexed expression clouding her countenance. "The words were on my lips, but I could not say them. I could not say anything at first; he quite took away my breath. When I was able to speak I was full of doubt. I do not know if I love him. I esteem him and admire him; he has genius and goodness, and I can understand how a woman might be very proud of his love; but when he asked me to marry him, it startled me and pained me, instead of — of making me very happy, you know."

Mr. Dent did not know at all; Prudence's insensibility and hesitation were simply incomprehensible to him; but he nodded his head appreciatively, as if he took in the whole situation.

"What did you say to him?"

"Almost what I am saying to you."

"But that was not a very definite answer to a proposal of marriage, it strikes me."

"I asked him not to refer to the subject again at present."

"That was dodging the question, Prue."

"I wanted time, uncle, to know my own mind."

In effect, Prudence had neither accepted nor rejected the young minister.

"Rather flattering for a man of Dillingham's character and position," thought Mr. Dent, "to be kept cooling his heels in an anteroom that way."

"You see, uncle, it was too important a step to be taken without reflection. Thoughtless persons should not be allowed to marry, ever."

"How long will it take you, Prue, to know your mind?"

"I don't know," she said restlessly; "a week — a month, perhaps."

"And in the meantime Dillingham will continue his visits here just the same?"

"Just the same. I arranged all that."

"Oh, you arranged all that?"

"Yes."

"But will it not be a little awkward for everybody?"

"I suppose so," said Prudence, looking wretched as she thought it over.

Mr. Dent was too wily to say anything more, for he saw that if Prudence was urged in her present wavering humor to give Dillingham a conclusive answer, it might possibly be in the negative.

However, the ice was broken, that was one point gained; the rest would naturally follow; for Prue could not long remain blind to the merits of a man like Dillingham, after knowing that he loved her. Mr. Dent laughed in his sleeve, thinking how sly it was in the young parson to corner Prue up there in the old fort, and attempt to carry her by storm. A vague exultation at Prue's not allowing herself to be taken in this sudden assault, formed, in spite of him, an ingredient in the good gentleman's merriment.

Mr. Dillingham passed the following evening at Willowbrook as though nothing unusual had occurred between him and Miss Palfrey. If the beggar maid, instead of accepting King Cophetua on the spot — as I suppose the minx did — had reserved her decision for a month or two to consider the matter, the king could not have behaved meanwhile with more tact and delicacy than Mr. Dillingham exercised on this evening and in his subsequent visits.

Prudence carefully but not ostensibly avoided being left alone with him, and there was none of that awkwardness or constraint attending the resumption of purely friendly intercourse which Mr. Dent had anticipated.

Observing that the young couple no longer rode horseback, Mr. Dent hastened the cure of his ankle, and the rides were resumed under his supervision; but the bridle-path leading to the old earthwork was tacitly ignored by all parties. Prudence and Mr. Dillingham had gone that road once too often if nothing was to come of it.

Mr. Dillingham retraced his steps so skilfully, and had come back with so good grace to the point from which he had diverged, that Prudence began to doubt if she had not dreamed that tender episode of the old fort, and to question if the old fort itself were not a figment. The whole scene and circumstance had become so unreal to her that one morning, riding alone, as she sometimes did now, she let Jenny turn into the rocky path leading to the crest of the hill, and secured ocular proof that the ruined earthwork at least was a fact. Standing there in the embrasure, she felt for an instant as if the young clergyman's hand rested on her own. That same evening Mr. Dillingham made it all seem like a delusion again by talking to her and smiling upon her just as he had done the month previously. But the recollection that he had asked her to be his wife, and that she had a response to make to the momentous question, now and then came over Prudence like a chill.

Rather vexatiously for Mr. Dent, somewhat restlessly for his ward, and perhaps not altogether happily for Mr. Dillingham — however composed he seemed — two weeks went by.

XV

COLONEL PEYTON TODHUNTER

At the end of those two weeks, Mr. Dillingham, who had not spoken to Mr. Dent relative to the position of affairs between himself and Prudence, took occasion to do so one December afternoon, as he was sitting with his friend before the open wood-fire in the library.

There is a quality in an open wood-fire that stimulates confidence ; it is easy, in the warm, mellow glow, to say what it would be impossible with other accessories to put into unreluctant words ; there is no place like an old-fashioned chimney-side in which to make love or to betray the secret of your bosom.

Mr. Dent was in an unusually receptive state for the young minister's confidence. The slow process by which Prudence was arriving at a knowledge of her own mind did not rhyme well with her guardian's impatience, and was beginning to depress him. He had expected, as a matter of course, that his friend Dillingham would seize the first opportunity, and he had given him several, to broach the subject; but two weeks had elapsed, and the young man had not spoken. Mr. Dent drew a distressing inference from this silence. Possibly while Prudence was pondering what to do, Mr. Dillingham was regretting what he had done. Mr. Dent ached to give the young minister an encouraging word; but he could not, without a sacrifice to his dignity, be the first to touch upon the topic. He desired above all things that Prudence should wed Dillingham, but he was not going to throw her at his head.

When Mr. Dillingham saw fit, then, this December afternoon, to break through his reticence, his friend welcomed the confidence eagerly. The younger man was gratified, but presumably not surprised, to find that Mr. Dent had his interests very much at heart.

"Nothing in the world, Dillingham, would make me happier," Mr. Dent was saying, with his hand resting on the young minister's shoulder, when Fanny came into the room and gave Mr. Dent a card.

"'Colonel Peyton Todhunter,'" Mr. Dent read aloud. "What an extraordinary name! Wants to see me? I don't know any Colonel Todhunter. Another subscription to the soldiers' fund, may be. Show him in, Fanny."

"Perhaps I had better withdraw," suggested Mr. Dillingham.

"Not at all; the gentleman will not detain me long, and I have a great deal to say to you."

Mr. Dillingham rose from the chair and walked to the farther part of the library, where he occupied himself in looking over a portfolio of Hogarth's prints. Presently Fanny, with a rather confused air, ushered in the visitor — a compactly built gentleman somewhat above the medium height, with closely cut hair, light whiskers and mustache, inclining to red, and a semi-military bearing. He wore, in fact, the undress uniform of an officer of artillery.

"Mr. Dent — Mr. Ralph Dent?" inquired this personage.

"Yes, sir; I am Mr. Ralph Dent."

"My name is Todhunter — Colonel Todhunter, of South Carolina."

Mr. Dent bowed somewhat formally, for he was an uncompromising Union man, and a South Carolinian colonel — a prisoner on parole, he supposed — was not a savory article to his nostrils.

"Of South Carolina?" repeated Mr. Dent, placing a chair at the colonel's disposal.

"Perhaps I ought to say, sir," said Colonel Todhunter, seating himself stiffly, "that I am in the United States army. I am one of the few West Point officers born in the South who have stuck to the old flag. Stuck to the old flag, sir."

Mr. Dent complimented him on his loyalty, and begged, with a slight access of suavity, to know how he could be of service to him.

"I come on very unhappy business; business of a domestic nature, sir," said the colonel, glowering at Mr. Dillingham as much as to say, "Who in the devil is that exceedingly lady-like young gentleman in the white choker?"

"Whatever your business is," said Mr. Dent, disturbed by this gloomy preamble, "do not hesitate to speak in the presence of my friend, the Rev. Mr. Dillingham. Mr. Dillingham, Colonel Todhunter."

The two gentlemen bowed distantly.

"I am the bearer of bad news for you, sir," said the colonel, turning to Mr. Dent. "Your nephew" —

"Gad, I knew it was Jack!" muttered Mr. Dent. "My nephew, Colonel Todhunter? I hope he is in no trouble."

"In very serious trouble, sir. In fact, sir, you must prepare yourself for the worst. In a skirmish with the enemy last month, near Rich Mountain, he was wounded and taken prisoner, and has since died. He was in my regiment, sir; the 10th Illinois."

Mr. Dent, who had partly risen from his

chair, sank back into the seat. Though Jack's letter, when it came a fortnight before, had annoyed him, he had been glad to know the boy was alive and well, more glad than he acknowledged to himself. The intelligence of Jack's death, dropping upon him like a shell from a mortar — for the colonel had acquitted himself of his duty with military brevity and precision — nearly prostrated Mr. Dent.

"Dear me, Dillingham," he said huskily, "this is very sad."

He sat for several moments without speaking, and then, recollecting his position as host, he begged the young minister to ring for Fanny and ask her to bring in some sherry and biscuits for the colonel.

Mr. Dent took a glass of the wine mechanically, which he held untasted in his hand, leaving it to Mr. Dillingham to entertain the stranger.

"Did I understand you to say you were from South Carolina?" asked Mr. Dillingham, breaking through the thin ice of his reserve.

"From South Carolina, sir," replied the colonel.

"That is also my State," said the young clergyman. "I am distantly connected by marriage with one branch of the Todhunters — the Randalls."

"I come from the Peyton branch, sir. I beg a hundred pardons, sir, but I did not quite catch your name when our afflicted friend did me the honor."

"Dillingham."

"Ah, yes, I recollect," said the colonel, fixing his eye abstractedly on the ceiling, and fingering his glass, "a Todhunter did marry a Dillingham; but it was one of the other branch. However, sir, delighted to make your acquaintance; delighted;" and Colonel Todhunter, who had not spared the sherry, shook hands effusively with Mr. Dillingham, who immediately froze over again.

The conversation between them still went on, with a difference, and the colonel explained how he came to be the bearer of the mournful news just delivered. Young Dent had joined his regiment only a short time before, but he had taken a liking to the young man; saw his ability with half an eye, sir. Was terribly cut up when the report came in that young Dent was hurt. Dent had mentioned the fact of his uncle living at Rivermouth, and the colonel, being at Boston on private affairs, determined to bring the information in person. The report of Dent's death in the rebel hospital — or rather in an ambulance, for he died on the way to the hospital, sir — had reached the colonel as he was on the point of starting for the North.

After this the conversation flagged; the colonel made several attempts to leave, but the decanter of sherry seemed to exert a baleful fascination over him. Finally he departed.

"Upon my word, Dillingham," said Mr. Dent, "this grieves me more than I can tell you."

"I can understand your sorrow," said Mr. Dillingham softly. "I once lost a nephew, and though he was only a child, and I was very young then, the impression lingered with me for years. It was my first knowledge of death."

"I have known death before," said Mr. Dent sadly; "it is always new and strange." Then after a long pause: "I would like to have your advice on one point, Dillingham. Years ago there was a slight love-passage between Prue and my nephew — a boy and girl love-affair, which amounted to nothing; but for all that, this news will affect Prue seriously — under the circumstances. I am certain of it. How can I tell her?"

"Is it necessary to inform her immediately?" asked Mr. Dillingham thoughtfully.

"I am afraid it is; there is, you know, a question of property involved."

"Of course," said Mr. Dillingham, "I would naturally advocate any step to shield Miss Palfrey from a thing likely to afflict her. So perhaps my judgment is not worth much; but suppose there should be some mistake in this? Colonel Todhunter's account, according to his own showing, is at second hand. It may or may not be authentic. Why take the darkest view of the case, while there is a chance to hope that he has been misinformed or deceived? Either of these things is likely. If I were entirely disinterested, I believe I should advise keeping this from Miss Palfrey as long as possible. In the meantime, with her mind undisturbed " —

"You are right; you are always right, Dillingham."

Mr. Dent grasped eagerly at the slight hope held out by the young minister's words. There was Lieutenant Goldstone, Goldstone's youngest son, reported killed at Big Bethel, reported officially; prayers were offered in church for the family, and they had gone into mourning, when young Goldstone announced himself at headquarters one day, having escaped through the Confederate lines. This and two or three similar instances occurred to Mr. Dent, and he began to be sanguine that the worst had not happened. It would be a remarkable thing, indeed, if Jack, after passing three years unscathed among the desperadoes of Montana and

California, should be killed within a week after setting foot on civilized ground, even in a state of war. Mr. Dent was one of those men who have the faculty of deferring the unpleasant, and seem, superficially considered, to be lacking in proper sensibility; while in fact it is the excess of sensibility that causes them to shrink, as long as may be, from facing what is disagreeable.

"Dillingham!" he exclaimed, looking up quickly, "I hope Colonel Todhunter will not spread this rumor in town. It would be dreadful for Prue to hear it unprepared. Stories fly so! I wish you would hunt up the colonel and caution him."

"I will," returned Mr. Dillingham, "and I will do it without delay. I confess, however, that nothing less urgent would induce me to continue his acquaintance. I was not favorably impressed by him."

"Nor I. He likes his sherry," observed Mr. Dent, glancing at the empty decanter, and smiling.

"Much too well," said Mr. Dillingham gravely.

The young minister lost no time in returning to the hotel, and the first person he met was Colonel Todhunter, who had been refreshing himself at the sample-room attached to

Odiorne's grocery. The colonel was in so boisterous a mood that it was not pleasant to confer with him in a public place like the doorway of the Old Bell Tavern, and Mr. Dillingham was obliged to invite the gentleman into the study.

During the four days he remained in town, Colonel Todhunter left very few sample-rooms unexplored. By sheer force of instinct, and seemingly without effort on his part, he went directly to every place where mixed drinks were obtainable. He made the acquaintance of everybody, spent his money with a lavish hand, and was continually saying, "Gentlemen, will you walk up and cool your coppers?" In less than twenty-four hours Colonel Peyton Todhunter was a marked character in Rivermouth, and stood deservedly high in the estimation of those gentlemen — mostly congregated at Odiorne's grocery — whose coppers required periodical cooling.

Jeremiah Bowditch was seen flitting about the streets at this period, in a state of high cerebral excitement. He became almost ubiquitous under the colonel's inspiration, and nearly accomplished the difficult task of taking two drinks at the same instant in two different sections of the town. Those were halcyon days for Mr. Bowditch.

Mr. Dillingham was grossly scandalized by the unseemly conduct of Colonel Todhunter, who, on the score of the far-off matrimonial alliance between their families, claimed a near relationship with the young minister, and insisted on dropping into his rooms at all hours of the day and night. "My Cousin James," he would remark, a little pompously, to the admiring circle in Odiorne's store, "has lost something of his hearty Southern manner since he came up North; but he's a good fellow at bottom." "Dill, my boy," he was overheard to say one night, when the young clergyman was vainly remonstrating with him on the staircase of the hotel — " Dill, my boy, you're a trump — you *are!*"

All this was very shocking, and for once the gentle face of Mr. Dillingham lost its serenity. The anxious, worn expression that came upon it showed how keenly he was suffering from the colonel's persecutions.

The day succeeding Colonel Todhunter's visit to Willowbrook Mr. Dent drove over to town to pay his respects to the colonel, if he had not already gone, and to interrogate him more explicitly as to the sources of his information concerning the unhappy tidings he had brought. At the interview the day before Mr. Dent had been too much distressed to inquire, as he afterwards wished to do, into the particulars of the case. The colonel was not in.

"Perhaps you are fortunate in not finding him," said Mr. Dillingham wearily. "He is drinking, and behaving himself in the most reckless manner. I have no doubt Colonel Todhunter is a warm-hearted, loyal person" — Mr. Dillingham would not speak unleavened evil of any one — "and in the South his free, liberal ways would be thought nothing of; but here they seem strange, to say the least, and I shall be heartily glad when he clears out."

"I hope he has not been indiscreet about Jack," said Mr. Dent uneasily.

"I do not think he has. I cautioned him, and he appeared to understand that he was not to mention the matter."

"But a man in his cups will talk."

"Still, I believe he has said nothing on the subject. I fancy he does not care enough about it. I trust to that for his silence rather than to his promise. I only wish he would go."

Mr. Dent went back to Willowbrook without seeing the colonel, who vanished from the town at the end of the week. But the fame of Colonel Peyton Todhunter was long kept green in Rivermouth — in the confused brain of Mr. Bowditch, and in the annals of Odiorne's grocery store, where the colonel had neglected to pay for numerous miscellaneous drinks. Fanny, the housemaid at Willowbrook, used to allude to him as "that merry gentleman," his merriment (as Fanny afterwards confessed to Wingate, the coachman) having expressed itself to her in a most astonishing wink just as she was ushering him that day into Mr. Dent's library. Against the dull background of New England life, the figure of the gay artillery officer stood out like a dash of scarlet in a twilight sky.

The gallant colonel had dawned on the Rivermouthians like the god Quetzalcoatl on the Aztecs, like Hiawatha on the Indian tribes of North America; and like them, also, he had departed mysteriously. A belief in his second coming, to inaugurate an era of gratuitous Jamaica rum, formed a creed all by itself among a select few. Mr. Odiorne was very anxious to have him come again; but his was a desire rather than a belief.

The more Mr. Dent reflected on Colonel Todhunter's visit, the more sceptical he grew on the subject of his nephew's death.

"He's a rattle-brained, worthless fellow," said Mr. Dent, meaning Colonel Todhunter, "and I don't believe a word of it. But what could possess him to come to me with such a story? What possesses people to do all sorts of mad things? May be it was a drunken freak of the colonel's; perhaps he intended to borrow money of me, and forgot to do so. Very likely he borrowed money of Dillingham. I'll ask him."

Colonel Todhunter *had* borrowed fifty dollars of the young clergyman. Mr. Dent enjoyed that.

"You may smile, my friend," said Mr. Dillingham, acknowledging the fact, "but I was not so blind a victim as you imagine. I attached a slight condition to the loan — that he should clear out on the instant. If he had suspected his strength he could have wrung ten times the sum from me. The colonel was an infliction, a positive agony, and I think I did very well to invest fifty dollars in his departure."

"You may rely upon it, Dillingham, that man was an impostor, and his purpose was money."

"I begin to fear so," said Mr. Dillingham. "It is disheartening to see a man of good average ability, like the colonel's, fallen so low."

Mr. Dent laughed, not at the unworldliness of the young clergyman — that was rather touching to Mr. Dent — but at the picture he had in his mind of the consternation and panic into which his friend must have been thrown

PRUDENCE PALFREY 215

by the insolent familiarity of the dashing Southern colonel during his sojourn at the Old Bell Tavern. The man had necessarily stayed at the same house, there being but one hotel in the town.

That Colonel Peyton Todhunter was an adventurer and a rascal was so excellent a key to the enigma of his raid on Rivermouth, that Mr. Dent in his heart forgave him, and felt rather under obligations to him for his moral turpitude. If the colonel had been a gentleman, Mr. Dent would have been forced to receive his communication in good faith; as it was, Mr. Dent was not going to give it the faintest credence.

"Must know Jack, though," Mr. Dent reflected; "must have known that Jack was not in the habit of writing to me, or the man would not have dared to come here with any such yarn. If the colonel is a sample of the friends Jack has picked up, I hope he has not picked up many."

The result of Mr. Dent's cogitations was that Colonel Todhunter's statement was a fabrication, at least the tragic part of it; the man must have had a general knowledge of Jack's antecedents and of his present surroundings, or he would not have been able to invent so plausible a story. The colonel was a bounty-agent, a camp hanger-on of some kind, and had come across Jack in the army. It was clear that Jack had carried out the intention, expressed in his letter to Twombly, to join the service; the rest was apocryphal.

Strengthened by Mr. Dillingham's view of the case, Mr. Dent concluded for the present to keep from Prudence the nature of Colonel Todhunter's visit, and also decided not to mention the letter which John Dent had written to Twombly. If it had not been for Parson Hawkins's will, Mr. Dent would have laid both matters before her now without hesitation; but he remembered how Prudence had recoiled at the mere suggestion of becoming John Dent's heir — it was not to be wondered at under the circumstances — and he lacked the courage to inform her of Colonel Todhunter's ridiculous report.

If Jack had actually been killed in action, it was not a difficult thing to obtain an official statement of the fact; if there was nothing in the story, it would be worse than useless to annoy Prue with it. The matrimonial question still remained open, and was sufficiently vexatious without other complications.

Prudence's capricious delay in making up her mind about Mr. Dillingham pressed more heavily each day on Mr. Dent. It was so unfair to Dillingham ; but what could he, Mr. Dent, do ? If he urged her to marry the young man, she would probably refuse. If he let matters take their own turn, they might be Heaven only knew how long in coming to a satisfactory end. In the meantime there was John Dent likely to be alive or likely to be dead at any moment.

Mr. Dent's was an open nature, and to be the repository of secrets weighed him down. His face was a dial on which the workings of the inner man were recorded with inconvenient accuracy. Prudence observed her guardian's perturbed state, and attributed it to her own perversity in not loving Mr. Dillingham on the spot.

Though Mr. Dent discredited the colonel's assertions, they troubled him ; but Prudence's procrastination troubled him more. Mr. Dillingham had borne it with noble patience, but he was obviously becoming restless under the suspense. A man may be a saint, yet, after all, there are circumstances under which a saint may be forgiven for recollecting that he is a man.

"I don't think Prue understands how painful this is for Dillingham," thought Mr. Dent. "She takes it very coolly herself. She was twice as much exercised the other day in deciding whether she should put a green or a purple stripe into an afghan. I never saw such a girl!"

Of the three persons concerned, Mr. Dent was perhaps the most worthy of commiseration, though Prudence was far from being as unruffled and happy as she had the grace to appear.

The conference between Mr. Dent and the young minister, interrupted by the apparition of Colonel Peyton Todhunter that winter afternoon, was resumed a few days subsequently, and was most satisfactory to both parties. Prue's conscientiousness, which amounted almost to a flaw in her character, explained her hesitation in responding to his young friend's wishes. (That was the way Mr. Dent put it.) When she did give him her heart, it would be a heart of gold, and would be given royally. Mr. Dillingham did not regard this extreme delicacy as a flaw in Miss Palfrey; on the contrary, it heightened his admiration for her, and he would await the event with as much patience as he could teach himself.

"By the bye, Dillingham," said the amiable tactician, "I got a letter this morning from the War Department. My nephew is not down on the pay-roll of the 10th Illinois. I wrote to them relative to Colonel Todhunter. The colonel of the 10th Illinois is — what's his name? — I declare it has slipped my mind; and there's no such person in the regiment as Todhunter. Practically, I suppose there are plenty of tod-hunters in the regiment, but they are not so named."

Mr. Dillingham smiled, as one smiles at the jokes of one's meditated father-in-law.

"And so the man really was an impostor?"

"Of course he was. I suspected it the instant I set eyes on him," said Mr. Dent unblushingly.

XVI

HOW PRUE SANG AULD ROBIN GRAY

When, months before, Mr. Dillingham's intimacy at Willowbrook had given rise to those cruel stories which made Prudence half wish the young minister would fall in love with her, that she might refuse him and prove how far she was from dying of blighted affections — at that time it had seemed a simple thing to Prudence to tell Mr. Dillingham that she valued his esteem very highly, that she wanted him always for her friend, but that she could never love him. One cannot be positive that she had not, in some idle moment, framed loosely in her thought a pretty little speech embodying these not entirely novel sentiments; but if this were the case, there was a difficulty now which she had not anticipated in the pronouncing of that little sentence.

Did she want to pronounce it? If such was to be the tenor of her reply to Mr. Dillingham, why had she not spoken the words that evening in the fort? There had been her time and chance to sweep all the Rivermouth gossips from the board with one wave of her hand, and so end the game. To be sure, Mr. Dillingham had confused her by the abruptness of his declaration; but she had recovered herself almost instantly, and ought to have been frank with him then and there. But she had been unable to give him an answer then, and now two weeks and more had slipped away, leaving her in the same abject state of indecision. Thus far Mr. Dillingham had shown to Prudence no sign of impatience; but her guardian was plainly harassed by her temporizing, and to Prudence herself the situation had grown intolerable.

She knew what her guardian's wishes were, though he had not expressed them, and his delicacy in not attempting to sway her influenced Prue greatly. She knew that her hesitation was adding to the disappointment and mortification Mr. Dillingham would have to face if she finally said No. He could but draw a happy augury from her delay; for if, in grammar, two negatives make an affirmative, in love, too much hesitation is equivalent to at least half a Yes. She was not certain that her vacillation had not made it imperative on her to accept his addresses. She stood aghast when she reflected that, without speaking a word, she had partly promised to be his wife.

The time when she could think lightly of putting aside his proffered love was gone; she shrunk now from the idea of giving him pain. Since Mr. Dillingham settled in Rivermouth her life had been very different, and if he passed out of it, as he must if she could not love him, the days would be blank again. Her esteem and friendship for him had deepened month by month, and during the past two weeks his bearing towards her, his deference, his patience, and his tenderness, had filled her with gratitude to him. There were moments when she felt impelled to go to him and place her hand in his, but some occult influence withheld her. There were other moments, for which she blamed herself, when the thought of him made her cold, a sense of aversion came over her — an inexplicable thing. Mr. Dillingham was so wise and noble and conscientious, there was no one with whom to compare him. He had the stable character, the brilliant trained intellect, all the sterling qualities, in short, that — that John Dent had not had. He was not arrogant, or impetuous, or light-minded, as John Dent had been : he had a singularly gentle and affectionate nature, and yet — and the absurdity of the fancy caused Prudence to laugh in the midst of her distractions — she could not imagine herself daring to call Mr. Dillingham "James." It was twice as easy to say "Jack!" even now. In her girlish love for *him* there had been none of these doubts and repulsions and conflicts. She had given him her whole heart, and had not known any better than to be happy about it. Why could she not do that now?

It was the oddest thing how, whenever she set herself to thinking of Mr. Dillingham, she thought of John Dent.

There was no one to whom Prudence could appeal for guidance out of the labyrinth into which she had strayed. Mr. Dent could not offer her unprejudiced counsel; she had an intuitive perception of the unfitness of her friend Veronica to help her, and the old parson was in his grave.

It was positively necessary that she should come to some determination soon; but she was as far away from it as ever that afternoon when these thoughts passed through her mind for the hundredth time.

"Let me think! let me think!" cried Prudence, walking up and down her room with a tortoise-shell dressing-comb rather unheroically in one hand. Unheroically? I suppose Ophelia twined those wild-flowers in her tresses with some care before she drowned herself. Medea and Clytemnestra would not make so graceful an end of it if they did not look a little to the folds of their drapery. One must eat, and drink, and dress, while life goes on. And if I show my poor little New England heroine in the act of putting up her back hair — it being nearly six o'clock, and Mr. Dillingham coming to tea — I feel that I am as true to nature as if I set her on a pedestal.

It was her chief beauty, that brown hair, and there were floods of it, with warm sparkles in it here and there, like those bits of gold-leaf that glimmer in a flask of Eau-de-vie de Dantzic when you shake it. She was arranging the hair, after the style of that period, in one massive braid over the brows, making a coronet which a duchess might have been proud to wear. The wonder of this braid was, it cost her nothing.

As Prudence set the last pin in its place, she regarded herself attentively for a moment in the cheval-glass, and smiled a queer little smile, noticing

"With half-unconscious eye,
She wore the colors he approved" —

a cherry ribbon at the throat and waist.

"I'm growing to be a fright," said Prudence, looking so unusually lovely that she could well afford to say it, as women always can — when they say it.

PRUDENCE PALFREY

There was a richer tint to her cheeks than ordinarily, and a deeper glow in her eyes this evening, and it did not escape the young minister, who, without seeming to see, saw everything.

When she came into the library where the two gentlemen sat, both were conscious of the brightness that surrounded her like an atmosphere. "Dillingham's fate is to be signed, sealed, and delivered to-night," was Mr. Dent's internal comment; "there is business in her eye." But poor Prue's brave looks sadly belied her irresolute, coward heart. She had no purpose but to look pretty, and that she accomplished without trying.

It was Mr. Dillingham's custom to leave Willowbrook at ten o'clock, unless there was other company ; then he kept later hours. There were no visitors on this occasion, and the evening appeared endless to Prudence, who paused absently in the midst of her sentences when the timepiece over the fireplace doled out the reluctant half-hours. It seemed to her as if ten o'clock had made up its mind not to come. Once or twice in the course of the evening the conversation flickered and went out curiously, as it was not in the habit of doing among these friends.

When the talk turns cold in this sort, it requires great tact to bury the corpse decently. Even with a gifted young divine to conduct the services, the ceremony is not always a success.

At half past nine Mr. Dent violated the tacit covenant that had existed between him and Prudence, by leaving her alone with Mr. Dillingham — for the first time since it had become embarrassing to be left alone with him. They had been discussing a stanza in Lowell's Vision of Sir Launfal, and Mr. Dent had coolly walked off to the library on a pretext to look up the correct reading.

Prudence regarded her guardian's action as a dreadful piece of treachery, and the transparency of it was perhaps plain to Mr. Dillingham, who came to her rescue, for an awkward silence had immediately fallen upon Prue, by requesting her to sing a certain air from Les Huguenots which she had been practising.

Prudence was in no humor for music, but she snatched at the proposition with a kind of gratitude, and sang the passage charmingly, with a malicious enjoyment, meanwhile, in the reflection that her recreant guardian, hearing the piano, would know that his purpose was frustrated. And in fact, at the first note that reached the library, there came over Mr. Dent's face an expression of mingled amusement and disgust, in strange contrast with the exquisite music that provoked it. He stood with one hand lifted to a book-shelf, and listened in a waiting attitude; but when the aria was finished, he made no motion to return to the drawing-room.

Prudence sat with her fingers playing in dumb show on the ivory keys, wondering what the next move would be. Mr. Dillingham, who had been turning over a portfolio of tattered sheet-music, took up a piece which he had selected from the collection, and came with it to the piano.

"I wish you would sing this, Miss Prudence. It is an old favorite of mine, and it is many years since I heard it. These homely Scotch ballads are not perhaps high art, but they have a pathos and an honesty in them which I confess to admiring."

As the young minister spoke he spread out on the piano-rack some yellowed pages containing the words and music of Auld Robin Gray.

Prudence gave a little start, and a peculiar look flitted across her face; then she dropped her eyes, and let her hands lie listlessly in her lap.

"But may be you don't sing it?" said Mr. Dillingham, catching her half-dreamy, half-pained expression.

"Oh, yes, I do," said Prudence, rousing herself with an effort, "if I have not forgotten the accompaniment."

She touched the keys softly, and the old air came back to her like a phantom out of the past. She played the accompaniment through twice, then her voice took up the sweet burden, half inaudibly at first, but gathering strength and precision as she went on. It was not a voice of great compass, but of pure quality and without a cold intonation in it. One has heard famous cantatrici, all art down to their fingernails, who could not sing a simple ballad as Prudence sang this, because they lacked the one nameless touch of nature that makes the whole world kin. "Young Jamie loo'd me weel," sang Prue —

"Young Jamie loo'd me weel, and socht me for his bride,
But saving a croun, he had naething else beside :
To mak' that croun a pund, young Jamie gaed to sea,
And the croun and the pund were baith for me.

"He hadna been awa a week but only twa,
When my mother she fell sick, and the cow was stown awa ;
My father brak his arm, and young Jamie at the sea,
And auld Robin Gray cam' a-courtin' me."

Mr. Dillingham, who understood music thoroughly, as he seemed to understand everything, listened to Prudence with a sort of wonder, though he had heard her sing many a time before. The strange tenderness and passion there was in her voice brought a flush to his pale cheek, as he leaned over the end of the piano, with his eyes upon her.

> "My father couldna work, and my mother couldna spin;
> I toiled day and nicht, but their bread I couldna win;
> Auld Rob maintained them baith, and wi' tears in his ee,
> Said, Jenny, for their sakes, O, marry me !
>
> "My heart it said nay, for I looked for Jamie back,
> But the wind it blew high, and the ship it was a wrack :
> The ship it was a wrack — why didna Jamie dee ?
> Or why do I live to say, Wae 's me ?
>
> "My father argued sair ; my mother didna speak ;
> But she lookit in my face till my heart was like to break :
> So they gied him my hand, though my heart was in the sea,
> And auld Robin Gray was gudeman to me."

It was with unconscious art that Prudence was rendering perfectly both the sentiment and the melody of the song, for her thought was far away from the singing. It was a day in midsummer ; the wind scarcely stirred the honey-suckles that clambered over the porch of the little cottage in Horseshoe Lane ; John Dent was telling her of his plans and his hopes and his love ; it was sunshine and shadow, and something sad ; again he was holding her hand ; she felt the touch of his lips on her cheek ; then she heard the gate close, and the robins chattering in the garden, and the tears welled up to Prue's eyes, as she sang, just as they had done that day when all this had really happened. And still the song went on —

> "I hadna been a wife a week but only four,
> When, sitting sae mournfully at the door,
> I saw my Jamie's wraith, for I couldna think it he,
> Till he said, I 'm come back for to marry thee.

> "O, sair did we greet, and muckle did we say;
> We took but ae kiss, and we tore ourselves away:
> I wish I were dead" —

Suddenly something grew thick in Prudence's throat; the dual existence she was leading came to an end, and the music died on her lip. She looked up, and met the young clergyman's eyes glowing upon her.

"I — I can't sing it, after all," she said, with a wan look. "I will sing it another time."

Then she pushed back the piano-stool abruptly, hesitated a moment, and glided swiftly out of the room.

Mr. Dillingham followed her with his eyes, much mystified, as he well might have been, at Prudence's inexplicable agitation and brusqueness. He leaned against the side of the piano, waiting for her to return; but she did not come back again to the drawing-room.

In a few minutes Mr. Dent appeared, and could scarcely control his astonishment at finding the young minister alone.

It was as plain to Mr. Dent as that one and one make two (though they sometimes refuse to be added together) that events had culminated during his absence. He had intended they should ; but there was a depressing heaviness in the atmosphere for which he was not prepared. He did not dare to ask what had happened.

Mr. Dillingham was ill at ease, and after one or two commonplace remarks, he said goodnight mechanically and withdrew.

" She has thrown him over, the foolish girl ! " muttered Mr. Dent, as he went gloomily upstairs with his bedroom candle in his hand, " and I am devilishly sorry."

It was clear that the young minister's fortunate star was not in the ascendant that night, when he asked Prue to sing Auld Robin Gray.

XVII

HOW MR. DILLINGHAM LOOKED OUT OF A WINDOW

It was a blustery, frosty morning; the sensitive twigs of trees snapped with the cold; the brass knockers on old-fashioned doors here and there had a sullen, vindictive look, daring you to take hold of them; the sky was slate-color. There was no snow on the ground, but the wind, sweeping up the street, now and then blew the white dust into blinding clouds, which, bursting in the air and sifting lazily downward, seemed to Mr. Dillingham, as he leaned against the casement of a window in the Old Bell Tavern, quite like falling snow.

The window at which the young minister stood was directly over the front door, and commanded a prospect of the entire length of the street that ran at right angles with the main thoroughfare and terminated at the steps of the hotel. At the other end of this street was the long bridge — hidden from time to time that morning by the swirls of dust — leading to Willowbrook.

Mr. Dillingham had his eyes fixed upon a distant object approaching from that direction. It was a mere speck when he first descried it on the bridge, tossed and blown hither and thither by the gale; but as it struggled onward he was not slow to detect in this atom the person of Mr. Dent's coachman, Wingate.

Not an especially interesting atom, Wingate, as a general thing, to the rest of the human family; but he interested Mr. Dillingham very deeply this morning.

As the coachman drew nearer, the young minister saw that he held something white clutched in his hand, which the marauding winds, now and then swooping down on him from around the corners, attempted to wrest from his grasp. That it was a note from Miss Palfrey, that it was for him, Mr. Dillingham, and that it contained the death-warrant of his hopes, were the conclusions at which he arrived before Wingate gained the stone-crossing opposite the hotel.

As Wingate reached this point, and was backing up against the wind which just then swept furiously around the paint-shop on the corner, a hack stopped suddenly on the crossway. A man leaned from the window, and called to Wingate, who stared at him stupidly for a moment, then rushed to the side of the carriage and grasped the hand of the occupant; then the two entered into an animated dialogue, if one might judge by the energetic pantomime that ensued.

Mr. Dillingham watched this encounter — evidently unexpected by both parties — with a feverish restlessness not characteristic of him. His breath came and went quickly, and his impatience seemed to take shape and become crystallized in eccentric zigzag lines on the pane of glass nearest his lips. It was rapidly growing bitter cold without, and the frost was stretching its silvery antennæ over all the windows.

Finally the carriage drove off, and Wingate, as if possessed to prolong the tantalizing suspense of the young clergyman, stood motionless on the curbstone several minutes looking after the retreating vehicle. Then it appeared to occur to Wingate that he was freezing to death, and he crossed over briskly to the Old Bell Tavern.

Mr. Dillingham hurried into the hall and snatched the note from the benumbed fingers of the astonished coachman, who was accustomed to much suavity and frequent fifty-cent pieces from the parson.

"All right — Wingate — thank you!" and the door was closed unceremoniously upon the messenger.

Dillingham watched

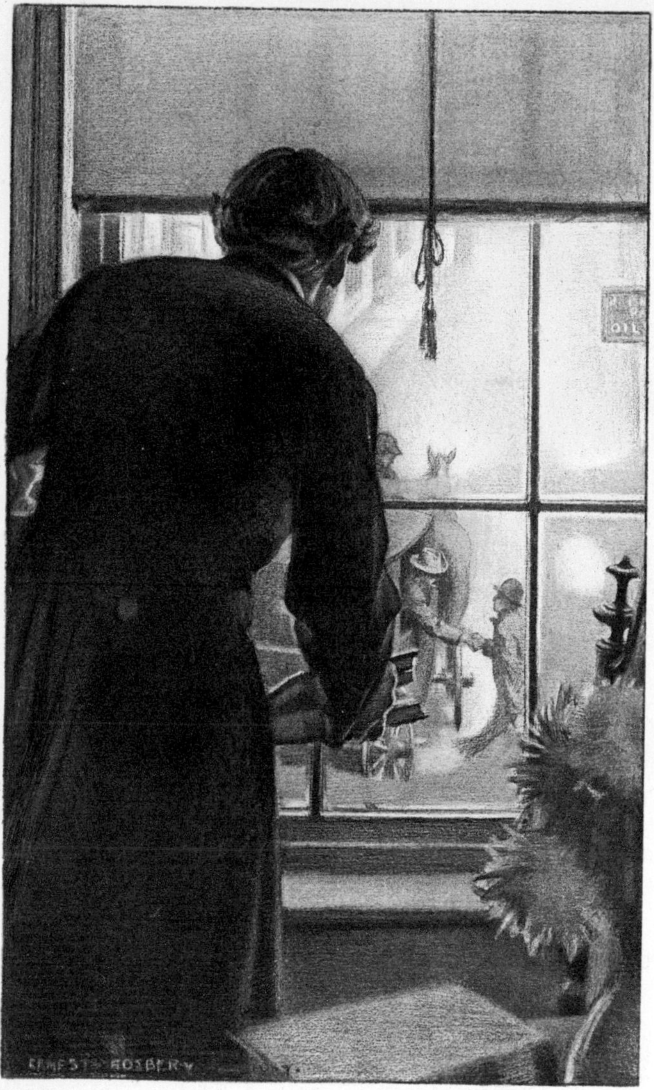
OIL

Mr. Dillingham broke the seal of the envelope, and read the note at a glance, for it was very brief. Directly after reading it he tore the paper into minute fragments, which he threw into the grate. The gesture with which he accompanied the action, rather than his face, betrayed strong emotion; for his face was composed now, and something almost like a smile played about his lips.

He stood for a few seconds irresolute in the middle of the apartment; then he went into the adjoining room, his sleeping-chamber, and took down his overcoat from a shelf in the black-walnut wardrobe.

This was the morning after Prue's musical failure. She had despatched the note to Mr. Dillingham as soon as breakfast was over, but it had been written long before. She had written it in the early gray of the morning — sitting in a ghostly way at her desk, wrapped in a white cashmere shawl, with her feet thrust into a pair of satin slippers of the Cinderella family, while the house slept. It was one of four letters. The first was six pages, this was sixteen lines — a lesson for scribblers.

While Wingate was on his way to town with the missive, Prudence was in her room summoning up the resolution to tell Mr. Dent what she had done. It was not a cheerful task to contemplate, remembering how unreasonable and angry he had been when she opposed his wishes before. She had an unclouded perception of the disappointment she was going to give him this time. It was pretty clear to her that he had set his heart on the marriage.

Mr. Dent was trying to read the morning paper, when the library door opened gently; he did not look up at once, supposing it was Bodge, the house-boy, bringing in the coals, or Prudence coming to tell him what he dreaded to know positively.

When he did look up he saw John Dent standing on the threshold and smiling upon him apologetically.

"Good God, Jack! is that you?" cried Mr. Dent, letting the paper slip in a heap to his knees.

"Yes, I — I have come back."

Mr. Dent was not a superstitious person, but he felt for may be ten seconds that that was an apparition standing over there in the doorway. And there was much in John Dent's aspect calculated to strengthen the impression.

He was worn and pale, as if he had just recovered from a long illness, or died of it; his cheeks were sunken, his eyes brilliant, and his unkempt black hair was blacker than midnight

PRUDENCE PALFREY

against his pallor. A shabby overcoat was thrown across one shoulder, concealing the left arm which he carried stiffly at his side. There was a squalor and a misery about him, heightened by his smile, that would have touched the compassion of a stranger. Mr. Dent was in a depressed mood that morning, and this woful figure of his nephew, standing there and smiling upon him like a thing out of the churchyard, nearly brought the tears to his eyes.

"Why, Jack, boy, how ill you are!"

"I am only tired," said John Dent, dropping into a chair; "that and the slight hurt I 've got."

"Yes, I heard about that."

"You heard about it?"

"To be sure I did."

"How could you have heard of it?"

"Colonel Todhunter brought the news. Gad! I 've done the colonel something of an injustice."

"Colonel Todhunter?"

"I did n't believe a word he said; but then he declared you were dead."

"Colonel Todhunter did?"

"Yes."

"I do not want to contradict Colonel Todhunter, for that would n't be polite," said John Dent, with one of his old smiles, "but I regret to state that I am not dead. Who *is* Colonel Todhunter, anyway?"

Mr. Dent stared at him.

"What! you don't know the colonel? the colonel knows you very well. He told us all about it; the skirmish, you know, in which you were wounded, and taken prisoner, and" — Here Mr. Dent paused, seeing by the vacuous expression of his nephew's face that the words were meaningless to him. "Dear me," he thought, "how very much broken up he is; his memory is wholly gone."

"Uncle Ralph," said John Dent, "I never heard of Colonel Todhunter until this moment; I have not been in the army; I have not been in any skirmish; and I have not been taken prisoner."

This was too calm and categorical a statement not to shake Mr. Dent a little in his suspicion that the speaker was laboring under some mental derangement.

"I have been wounded, to be sure," continued John Dent. "I was shot in Western Virginia, in the woods, on my way to join the army — shot by George Nevins," he added between his teeth. "I imagine he got tired of me at last, and concluded to kill me. He failed this time; but he will do it, if that is his purpose."

In reading John Dent's letter to Joseph

Twombly, Mr. Dent had smiled at what he considered Jack's hallucination touching the watch which he supposed Nevins was keeping over him night and day; but this attempt on Jack's life, if there had really been one, at a spot so remote from the scene of the robbery three years before, gave a hue of probability to the idea.

Mr. Dent looked out of the corner of his eye at his nephew. Perhaps Jack *was* insane. Mr. Dent's faith in the general correctness of the colonel's statements was coming back to him. Sitting with his arms hanging at his side and his head resting on his chest broodingly, Jack seemed like a person not quite right in his mind.

"Where is this Colonel Todhunter?" he exclaimed, starting to his feet.

"Good heavens! don't be so violent!"

"Where is he, I say?"

"How can I tell? The man's gone."

"How long since?"

"A fortnight ago."

"Was he here — in this house?"

"He came here one afternoon, representing himself as your friend; he stayed in the town four or five days after that, I believe."

"It is three weeks since I was shot," said John Dent, reflecting. "Did Twombly see him?"

"I really can't say whether the deacon saw him or not."

"I don't mean the deacon, I mean Joe."

"Joseph was in Chicago; been there these six months."

"Uncle, what kind of person was this Colonel Todhunter? Describe him to me."

"He was something of a character, I should say; a cool customer; he made himself very much at home — with my sherry."

"Very gentlemanly, and rather pale?"

"Well, the sherry was pale," returned Mr. Dent, laughing, "but the colonel was rather florid and not at all gentlemanly; that is to say, he carried it with a high hand in the town, though he behaved decently enough when he called on me."

"What was he like?"

"A tall man, taller than you, for instance; strongly built, with blue eyes and long sandy whiskers."

"GEORGE NEVINS!"

"Nonsense!" said Mr. Dent.

"It was George Nevins, I tell you!"

"Pooh! you're mad. What would bring him here, of all the places in the world?"

"I don't know; there are many things I cannot fathom; but this I do know, you have stood face to face with the most daring and

PRUDENCE PALFREY

accomplished scoundrel that lives. There is n't his match in California or Nevada."

"Good heavens!" ejaculated Mr. Dent uneasily, with a sensation of having two or three bullet-holes in the small of his back. "You don't really believe that that man was the fellow Nevins?"

"I do, assuredly. He thought he had disposed of me, and he came here prospecting. It was like his impudence. He told you I was dead? Well, he had good reason to suppose so."

"I can't believe it. Gad, I don't believe it! If it had been he, I think I should have turned desperado instinctively, and brought him down with the old shot-gun;" and Mr. Dent was making a motion to that nearly harmless weapon, which had hung for years unloaded over the library mantelpiece, when Prudence walked into the room.

"Drop Colonel Todhunter," whispered Mr. Dent hastily.

XVIII

AN EMPTY NEST

PRUDENCE neither started nor fainted when she found John Dent with her uncle; she had seen John Dent descend from the hack at the gate ten or fifteen minutes previously — perhaps it gave her a turn at the instant — and she had now come to welcome him home. Nothing could have been more simple or natural than the meeting between them.

"I am glad to see you, Cousin John," said Prudence simply, as if she had parted with him yesterday, and had not eaten three thousand two hundred and eighty-five meals since that day when he failed to come back to dinner.

Prudence was unaffectedly glad to see John Dent; and the sincere friendliness of her greeting placed him at his ease. He had much to tell of his wanderings, and much to be told of Rivermouth affairs; and very soon the conversation flowed on between these three with only the slightest undercurrent of constraint. Indeed, it seemed to Prudence like that first day, long ago, when John Dent came to Rivermouth and surprised her by being a frank, light-hearted young fellow, instead of the mousing Dryasdust she expected. As in that time also, he had come to remain only a brief period; there were dragons still at large and giants yet unslain. As soon as his arm was well, he would bid good-by again to Rivermouth. The gold he was going in quest of now was that small quantity of bullion which is to be found in a lieutenant's shoulder-straps.

The parallel between his two visits occurred to John Dent himself, as he sat there chatting; and so far as his impecuniosity went, the parallel was too close to be agreeable. Before, he had had only a slender outfit and a few hundred dollars; and now he was the possessor of a navy revolver, and a suit of clothes which his uncle eyed thoughtfully from time to time, and resolved to have buried in the back garden at no remote period.

But in spite of this, a blissful serenity, born of the home-like atmosphere he was breathing, took possession of John Dent. His misfortunes were visions and chimeras; he was as a man who, awaking from a nightmare, finds himself in a comfortable warm room with the daylight pouring through the windows, and strives in vain to recollect the dream that a moment ago appalled him.

He looked so shabby, and uncared for, and happy, that Prudence was touched. In speaking of Parson Wibird, she was obliged to exert all her self-control not to tell John Dent of the legacy. Whatever he did, he should not go away until he was informed of that. She lingered on the subject of the parson's death, and came back to it at intervals, with the hope that her guardian would be tempted to break through the now slightly binding condition of the will. But the old parson recalled to Mr. Dent's mind the new parson, and he broke out, with that fine tact which characterized him, "By the way, Jack, you must know Dillingham; he's a capital fellow."

John Dent had learned from Wingate, in their hurried conference at the street corner, that Prudence was still unmarried; and for the moment he had forgotten everything save the delicious fact that he and Prue were sitting and talking together as of old. But now his countenance fell.

"I shall be glad to know him," he contrived to say, with more or less enthusiasm.

With this, Mr. Dillingham passed out of the conversation, and did not drift into it again. No other unfortunate word or allusion ruffled the tranquillity of that morning, which made way with itself so quickly that Fanny caused a sensation when she announced dinner.

The afternoon showed a similar suicidal tendency; and shortly after tea, John Dent, who began to feel the reaction of the excitement he had undergone, went to bed in the same room where he had slept three years before.

Apparently not a piece of the ancient mahogany furniture, which resolved itself, wherever it was practicable, into carven claws grasping tarnished gilt balls, had been moved since he was last there. It struck him, while undressing, that it would be only the proper thing for him to go around the chamber and shake hands with all the friendly old-fashioned paws — they stretched themselves out from tables and chairs and wardrobes with such a faithful, brute-like air of welcome.

The castellated four-post bedstead, with its snowy dimity battlements, seemed an incredible thing to John Dent as he stood and looked at it in the weird winter moonlight. It was many a month since he had lain in such a sumptuous affair.

A sensuous calm stole over his limbs when he stretched himself on the pliant springs of the mattress; then the impossible blue canaries, pecking at the green roses on the wall-paper, lulled him to sleep, and would have hopped down from the twigs and covered him with leaves, as the robins covered the babes in the wood, if he had not been amply protected by a great silk patch-quilt, deftly done into variegated squares and triangles by Prue's own fingers.

He slept the sleep of the just that night; he was a failure, but he slept the sleep of success; and his uncle, in the next room, dropped off with the soothing reflection that events had proved his wisdom in not telling Prue anything about Colonel Peyton Todhunter; but Prudence scarcely slept at all.

John Dent's wound was of the slightest, and the stiffness had nearly gone out of his shoulder when he awoke the next morning. He awoke in the same state of beatitude in which he had fallen asleep.

"I know I don't amount to much when I'm added up," he said, smiling at himself in the glass as if he enjoyed representing a very small vulgar fraction in the sum of human happiness; "but I am not going to trouble myself about it any more. I'll go down to Virginia, and come back presently with one leg and a pension, and spend the rest of my days telling stories to Prue's little ones." And John Dent sighed cheerfully as he pictured himself a gray-haired, dilapidated captain, or may be colonel, with two or three small Dillinghams clinging to his coat-skirts.

PRUDENCE PALFREY

It was a singular coincidence that both uncle and nephew should have reached that philosophical stage when they could look calmly on the prospect of playing grandfather and godfather respectively to Prue's children.

John Dent descended, and found Prudence and his uncle in the library, making a pretty domestic picture, with the wood-fire blazing cheerily on the hearth, lighting up the red damask curtains, and the snow outside dashing itself silently in great feathery flakes against the windows. It was like an interior by Boughton, with that glimpse of bleak winter at the casements.

"Good-morning," said John Dent, enveloping the pair in one voluminous smile.

"Good-morning, Jack," returned Mr. Dent, and "Good-morning, Cousin John," said Prudence, who hurried off to see to breakfast, for the Prodigal was to have a plate of those sublimated waffles of which only Prudence knew the secret. The art of their composition was guarded at Willowbrook as the monks in the Old World convents guard the distillation of their famous cordials.

The young man saw that he had interrupted a conversation between his uncle and Prudence, and experienced that uncomfortable glow about the ears which comes over one when the dialogue stops instantly at one's appearance.

However, as Prudence departed to superintend the serving up of the fatted waffle, John Dent drew a chair towards the fireplace and was about to seat himself, when his eyes fell upon a small cabinet photograph which rested against a vase at one end of the mantelpiece.

The back of the chair slipped from John Dent's fingers, and he stood, transfixed for a moment, looking at the picture; then he approached the mantel-shelf and took the photograph in his hand.

"Who is this?" he asked quickly; and he pointed a quivering finger at the face.

"That? why, that's my friend Dillingham, a cap—"

"Dillingham be ——!" cried John Dent. "That is George Nevins!"

Mr. Dent leaned back in his chair and suppressed himself.

"Quiet yourself," he said soothingly. "You have n't slept well, you"—

"Do you suppose I don't know that face!"

"That is just precisely what I suppose," cried Mr. Dent, giving way to his irritation, "and I could n't have expressed it better."

"Not know it! Have n't I thought of it every day for two years, fallen asleep thinking of it every night, dreamed of it a thousand times? He has cut his mustache and beard," said John Dent slowly and to himself, "and wears no collar to his coat. What — what is this doing *here?*" he cried, with sudden fury.

"Why, Jack, my boy, I tell you that that is the Rev. James Dillingham, the pastor of the Old Brick Church, Prue's friend and mine."

"You can't mean it!"

"Don't be an idiot. If you discover any resemblance to Colonel Todhunter in that picture, you 've a fine eye for resemblance."

"Todhunter was not the man," cried John Dent. "*This* is the man!"

It was patent now to Mr. Dent that his nephew was a monomaniac on the subject of George Nevins. First it had been Colonel Todhunter, now it was Dillingham, and by and by it would be somebody else, Prue or himself possibly. Mr. Dent coughed, and restrained the impatient words that rose to his lips. The boy's mind was turned by his misfortunes, and yet he seemed rational enough on other topics.

"You think I am crazy?" said the young man, reading his uncle's open countenance as if it were a book. "Well, I am not. I am as sane as you are, and as clear in the head as a bell. How long has your friend Mr. Dillingham been settled over the Brick Church?" and John Dent seated himself, crossing his legs comfortably, with the aspect of a man who is going to take things philosophically and not fret himself about trifles.

"Since last June," returned Mr. Dent, relieved to see his nephew calm again. "Dillingham came here in the latter part of May, and it is now December. Consequently he has been here a little over six months."

"While I was at Shasta," muttered the young man. "But who fired on me in Virginia, if it was n't Nevins?" Then in a negligent way to his uncle, "Where does your friend Dillingham live?"

"In Rivermouth, of course."

"Where?"

"At the Old Bell Tavern."

John Dent went out of the room like a flash.

After an instant of panic, Mr. Dent dashed after him. The hall door was locked and bolted; there was a complicated bolt with a chain, and the young man was tugging at the chain when his uncle seized him by the arm.

"What are you trying to do?"

"I must see this man Dillingham, Uncle Ralph."

"Certainly, so you shall see Dillingham. Ten to one he will ride out here before the morning is over, in spite of the storm; and then you will discover how absurd you are."

"Granting I am wrong," said John Dent as

composedly as he could, "I cannot wait to have proof of it. If he is the man I think he is, he knows where I am by this time, and will not show his face here. I must go to him."

"Before breakfast?"

"This instant!"

Mr. Dent reflected that perhaps the only cure for his nephew's delusion was to bring him face to face with the young minister, whom, by the way, Mr. Dent himself was anxious to see; he was still ignorant of what had passed in the drawing-room two nights previously, for Prudence had found no fitting moment since John Dent's arrival to inform her guardian of her decision and the letter she had written to Mr. Dillingham.

So one of the carriage horses was ordered to be harnessed to the buggy and driven around to the side door. Meanwhile John Dent paced the hall chafing; and Prudence, with her eyebrows raised into interrogation points, stood behind the coffee-urn in the breakfast-room, wondering what it all meant.

When the buggy was ready, Mr. Dent proposed to go to town alone and bring the young minister back with him; but John Dent would not listen to the suggestion, and the two drove off together in the storm.

The snow beat so persistently in their faces

all the way, that there was no chance for conversation, if either had been disposed to talk. Mr. Dent stole a glance now and then at the young man, whose eyes glowed wickedly over a huge white mustache which he had got riding in the teeth of the wind. "I've half a mind to tip the pair of us over the next bank," muttered Mr. Dent; "he's as mad as a March hare!"

On driving up to the door of the Old Bell Tavern, Mr. Dent begged his nephew to control himself and do nothing rash. John Dent promised this, but with set teeth and in a manner not reassuring.

"You are making a dreadful mistake; and if you involve me in any absurdity I'll never forgive you. Dillingham is my friend, and one of the noblest fellows in the world. It is rather early for a call; I'll go up first, Jack."

"And I'll go with you," said John Dent, with disgusting promptness.

Mr. Dillingham's suite of rooms was on the second floor, and the door of his parlor or study gave upon the main staircase. Mr. Dent, inwardly consigning his nephew to the shades below, knocked two or three times without awakening the well-known voice which always said "Come in" to his recognized knock; then he turned the handle of the door which was not fastened.

"He's in bed at this hour, of course," he remarked. The town clock was striking eight. "We'll step into his parlor and wait for him."

The room was in the greatest disorder; the drawers of a large escritoire between the windows were standing wide open, the grate was full of dead ashes, and over the carpet everywhere were scattered half-torn letters and papers. John Dent cast one glance around the apartment, and then rushed into the small bedchamber adjoining. The bed was unrumpled.

"Gone!" moaned John Dent, dropping into a chair.

"Gone? nonsense. Gone to breakfast," said Mr. Dent.

"It's no use," said the young man, settling himself gloomily in the chair; "he is hundreds of miles away by this time. While we were sitting in the chimney-corner over yonder, fire and steam and all infernal powers were whisking him off beyond my reach."

Mr. Dent pulled at the bell-cord as if he had suddenly had a bite, and jerked in Larkin the waiter. Where was Mr. Dillingham? Larkin did not know where Mr. Dillingham was. He would inquire at the office.

He returned shortly with the information that Mr. Dillingham had gone out quite early the day before, and had not been in since.

The young minister was in the habit of absenting himself for several days together without notifying the office-clerk, who supposed in this instance, as in the others, that Mr. Dillingham was visiting his friend Mr. Dent at Willowbrook.

"That 'll do, Larkin," said Mr. Dent. "Nothing particular. We 'll look in again."

Exit Larkin, lined with profanity.

Mr. Dent, with a feeble smile on his lips, stood looking at his nephew.

"It is too late," said the young man, "but I would like to send a telegram to Boston and one to New York."

"To whom?"

"To the chief of police."

Mr. Dent started. "Don't you do it! I know you are wrong, though I acknowledge that the thing has a strange look. You would feel rather flat if, after you had sent off a couple of libellous messages, Dillingham should turn up and explain it all in a dozen words, as I am positive he will. I could never look him in the face again."

"You won't, anyway," said John Dent. "However, I don't want to use the name of Dillingham in the matter. I shall simply give a description of the person of George Nevins. That will not inconvenience any one, I 'm afraid. See how he slips through my fingers! I should call the man an eel, if he was n't a devil."

Mr. Dent made no further objection; the two descended to the street and drove to the telegraph-office.

In the midst of writing a despatch, young Dent paused and nibbled the top of the pen-holder. "I wonder I did n't think of that before," he said to himself; and then in a low voice to his uncle, "Ask the operator if Dillingham has sent or received anything over the wires lately."

Mr. Dillingham had sent two telegrams the day before.

"Will you allow me to look at them a moment?"

Knowing Mr. Dent to be the intimate friend of the young pastor, the clerk obligingly took the copies of the two despatches from a clip on his desk and handed them to the elderly gentleman.

Dropping the date, the telegrams read as follows —

I

To Rawlings & Sons, Bankers, Chicago, Illinois:

Place the balance due me on account, and the six U. S. bonds you hold for me, to the credit and subject to the order of Colonel Peyton Todhunter.

JAMES DILLINGHAM.

II

To Colonel Peyton Todhunter, Milwaukee, Wisconsin:

Go to Chicago instantly. Draw funds from Rawlings. Will join you at 6666. You have failed. He is here. J. D.

"Are you convinced now?" whispered John Dent, having with breathless interest read these documents over his uncle's shoulder. "It appears, though I don't understand the last telegram at all, that your friend Colonel Peyton Todhunter is the friend of your worthy friend the Rev. James Dillingham; and a precious pair they are, if I may say so without hurting your feelings. 'He is here' means me of course; but what is meant by 'You have failed'? '6666' evidently designates some point of rendezvous."

"Jack," whispered Mr. Dent thickly, "I can't believe my eyes!"

"I would n't," said Jack. "I'd stand it out. In the meantime I will send off this description, and then we'll go back to the hotel. He decamped in haste, and may have left behind him something in the way of letters or papers that will be useful to me."

The young man seated himself at a desk, and, after a moment's reflection, wrote the following message, which he handed to his uncle —

MESSRS. RAWLINGS & SONS, Chicago, Ill. :

Has Colonel Todhunter drawn the funds described in the despatch of yesterday? If not, stop payment until further advices.

J. D.

"That's a clever idea," said Mr. Dent, awaking from the stupor that had fallen upon him. "We will have an injunction on them, if it is not too late; but isn't it a sort of forgery to use Dillingham's name this way?"

"I haven't used his name," answered Jack, laughing; "I have put my own initials to the document, like a man. Are you working through?" he asked, turning to the clerk. "Then send this along."

He resumed his seat at the desk, and fell to work on a personal description of George Nevins. This was a task of some difficulty, requiring a conciseness and clearness of diction which cost him considerable trouble. More than half an hour elapsed before John Dent had completed the portrait to his satisfaction. He was in the midst of his second despatch, when the operator received from Rawlings & Sons a telegram that seemed to puzzle him somewhat.

"This appears to be an answer to your despatch, sir, but it is addressed to Mr. Dillingham."

"A mistake at the other end," said Mr. Dent quickly.

"What do they say?" asked John Dent, reaching forward to take the long narrow strip of paper from the clerk's hand.

Colonel Todhunter had drawn out the funds in full. The Messrs. Rawlings & Sons trusted there was nothing wrong in the matter; they had acted strictly according to instructions.

"Just as I expected," said Jack, tossing the paper to his uncle, "luck is dead against me." Then he went on with his writing: "Five feet eight or nine inches; blue eyes; light hair, probably cut close; no beard or mustache" — etc., etc.

"This is simply horrible," murmured Mr. Dent; and as he walked nervously up and down the office, he recalled the afternoon when he introduced Dillingham to Colonel Todhunter, and how they had saluted each other as strangers, and appeared to dislike each other, being such different men; then he reflected that it was chiefly through his own means that this scandal had been brought upon Rivermouth; then he thought of Prue, and he turned cold and hot, and pale and flushed, by turns; and the rapid scratching of John Dent's pen over the paper, and the monotonous clicking of the satanic little telegraph instrument behind the wire screen, drove him nearly distracted.

"And now, if you please, we will inspect the sanctum sanctorum of the late incumbent," said John Dent gayly.

It was only human that he should relish the consternation of his uncle. But as they were passing out into the street, John Dent's face underwent a change; he halted on the last of the three steps leading to the sidewalk, and, grasping the iron railing, seemed unable to move further.

"What is it now?" asked Mr. Dent nervously.

"Uncle Ralph, was Prue engaged to that man? — did she love him?"

"No!" cried Mr. Dent; "I believe she hated him instinctively — thank God!"

"Amen!" said John Dent, drawing a long breath. "He has got my money, he has blighted two years of my life, but if he has n't got at the pure gold of Prue's heart, I forgive him!"

XIX

A RIVERMOUTH MYSTERY

The two Dents returned in silence to the Old Bell Tavern, and went up directly to the deserted study.

"First of all," said John Dent, closing the door and turning the key, "I want to know how he came here, how he managed to step into Parson Hawkins's shoes, and all the details. Tell me slowly, for I feel I shall not comprehend this thing, unless it is put in the simplest way."

The story of Mr. Dent's acquaintance with Dillingham in New York, and the chain of commonplace events that had ended in his coming to Rivermouth as the pastor of the Old Brick Church, was told in a few words. It was not a strange story, taking it link by link; it was only as a whole that it appeared incredible.

"He was an artist, that man," said Mr. Dent, with an involuntary pang of admiration, as he recalled the cleverness with which Dillingham had put Joseph Twombly out of the way. He recollected now that Dillingham had withheld his consent to come to Rivermouth until the very day Twombly started for Chicago. "Ah, Jack, if good people, as a class, were one half as intelligent and energetic as rogues, what a world this would be!"

"Knowing Nevins as I do," said John Dent when his uncle had finished, "his adroitness and cunning, I can understand what a tempting thing it was to him to play at this masquerade; but he must have had a deeper motive than a mere whim to keep him here seven months."

"He fell in love with Prue, of course," said Mr. Dent, with a twinge; "and then— I see it all, Jack! you were right. He *did* have a watch set on you; he meant to marry Prue, and keep you out of the parson's money, even if he had to kill you to do it! — it was Todhunter who made the attempt on your life when they saw you were coming East; it was Todhunter who dogged your steps all the time!"

"The parson's money?" said John Dent.

The words had escaped Mr. Dent in his excitement, as the whole of the desperate game which Dillingham had probably been playing flashed upon him. It will be remembered that on the morning when Parson Hawkins's later will was found, Mr. Dent went to Boston to meet Mr. Dillingham and conduct him to Rivermouth. Mr. Dent was full of the matter, and that night, at the Revere House, he had spoken freely to his friend of the old parson's whimsical testament. Perhaps it was in that same hour Dillingham formed the purpose to possess himself of the money — admitting, for the moment, that Dillingham was George Nevins.

John Dent stood looking inquiringly at his uncle. It was too late to recall the words; the circumstances seemed to warrant Mr. Dent now in disregarding the restriction of the will, and he told his nephew of the legacy.

At another moment, this undreamed-of fortune would have filled John Dent's heart with both joy and sadness; but the day, scarcely begun, had been too crowded with other emotions for him to give way to either now. He walked to the window and, rubbing a clear space on one of the panes, looked out into the snowy street for several minutes; then he turned to Mr. Dent and said quietly, "Let us look through these things."

A closer examination of the study and sleeping-room afforded indubitable evidence that the late occupant had abandoned them in desperate haste, but also that he had left behind him no letters or written memoranda giving any clue to his intended movements. A quantity of papers had been burnt in the grate; an undecipherable fragment of the note Prudence had written him lay on the hearth-rug, and near it the back of a delicate pink envelope with which no one would have thought of associating the fair Veronica if it had not borne her pretty monogram.

Mr. Dillingham had, so to speak, spiked his guns; but a company of embroidered worsted slippers — as gay as a company of Zouaves — and a number of highly mounted dressing-gowns sufficient properly to officer this metaphorical detachment, fell into the hands of the enemy.

The younger man, on his side, conducted the investigation with relentless scrutiny; but Mr. Dent only cursorily, for the place in his heart which Dillingham had occupied was yet warm with the late presence.

Two discoveries were made, unimportant in themselves, but one of which interested the nephew, and the other startled the uncle, who, in the progress of the search, appeared to be receiving a series of shocks from an invisible galvanic battery.

"Here's a photograph which was lost some time ago with a certain pocket-book containing a small sum of money;" and John Dent held out at arm's length a faded vignette head of Prudence, gazing at it thoughtfully. "The finder would have been liberally rewarded if I had got hold of him. Hullo! what's this? Somebody's bracelet," he added, fishing up a piece of jewelry from the depths of the travelling-trunk over which he was stooping.

"Dear, dear!" groaned Mr. Dent. It was Veronica Blydenburgh's bracelet. He knew of its loss; everybody knew of it. You could no more lose a bracelet in Rivermouth without everybody knowing it than you could lose your head.

This affair seemed blacker to Mr. Dent than all the rest — blacker than the attempt on Jack's life, inasmuch as petty larceny lacks the dignity of assassination. But I fancy Mr. Dent was a trifle uncharitable here. As a reminiscence of a lovely white wrist, the trinket may have had a value to Mr. Dillingham which Mr. Dent did not suspect.

"What a finished rogue he was! It is only when a man adds hypocrisy to his rascality, that he becomes a perfect knave."

"Yes," said John Dent, "that little lamb's-skin does aggravate the offence."

Mr. Dent walked off to the other end of the room and began turning over a lot of books and pamphlets piled in one corner.

"Look here, Jack!" he cried presently,

"here is where he got his sermons from — South's Sermons, Robertson's Sermons, Hooker's Sermons, Cumming's Great Tribulation, Peabody's Discourses. Gad! he mixed them up, old and young. By heaven! here's the very passage Prue thought so affecting Fast Day. See where he's changed 'London' into *Rivermouth*, and 'our Gracious Queen' into *our honored Chief Executive*. Jack," said Mr. Dent solemnly, "let us go home!"

"Uncle Ralph, that is almost the only rational suggestion you have made to-day. I am famished."

"And I am frozen," said Mr. Dent, with a shiver, picking up his overcoat. He drew on one sleeve, and paused.

"Well?" said his nephew.

"Jack, this thing must be hushed up, for Prue's sake. The deacons will have to know the truth, and may be one or two outsiders; but the townsfolk must never be allowed to suspect the real character of that man. Some plausible explanation of his flight must be circulated. If he has left any bills," continued Mr. Dent, with an unconscious grimace, "I shall pay them. I cannot eat a mouthful until this is settled. I must see Blydenburgh and Twombly and Wendell without wasting a moment, and I want you to come with me."

"For Prue's sake, and for your sake," said John Dent, laughing.

"Yes, for my sake too. Don't be hard on a fallen brother. You can't afford to, Jack. If Dillingham deceived me, George Nevins was too many for you."

"That's a fact," said John Dent.

In the course of an hour the deacons and trustees of the Old Brick Church assembled together mysteriously in Deacon Twombly's parlor — five or six honest, elderly, bald-headed gentlemen, who now had the air of dark-browed conspirators on the eve of touching off innumerable barrels of gunpowder. Deacon Zeb Twombly might have been taken for Guy Fawkes himself.

The next day it was known that the Rev. Mr. Dillingham had quitted Rivermouth; it was understood in the parish and in the town that family matters, involving the jeopardy of large estates, had called Mr. Dillingham away so suddenly that he had had time to advise only his immediate friends of his departure. It was also understood that his return was problematical. There were dark hints and whispers and rumors and speculations, to be sure; but for once a secret was kept in Rivermouth — though one woman knew it!

Prudence had to be told, of course, and she

nearly died with desire one afternoon, six months afterwards, to tell Veronica Blydenburgh everything — the afternoon Veronica came to her and said —

"Only think, Prue, papa found my opal bracelet under the flooring of the old summerhouse."

Veronica sat silent for a moment, dreamily weaving the bright coil in and out her slender fingers; then suddenly lifting her head, she cried —

"Prue, will you swear never to breathe it to a living soul if I tell you something?"

"Yes," said Prudence, with a start.

"Well, then, the afternoon before he went away so strangely" —

"Who went away?"

"Mr. Dillingham."

"Oh!"

"The afternoon before he went away, he — he offered himself to me."

"What!" cried Prudence, turning white and red. It was beginning to appear that Cupid had had two strings to his bow.

"I say," repeated Veronica, "that Mr. Dillingham offered himself to me."

"And you refused him!"

"O Prue! that's the bitterness of it! — I accepted him!"

The reader shall become my collaborator at this point and finish the romance to his own liking. It is only fair for me to inform him, however, that one morning last spring as I was passing, portmanteau in hand, from the station at Rivermouth to the old gambrel-roofed house in a neighboring street where I always find welcome, I saw a little man swinging on a gate.

I had never seen this small personage before, but there was something absurdly familiar in the dark hair and alert black eyes, something absurdly familiar in the lithe, wiry figure (it was as if John Dent had been cut down from five feet eight to three feet four); and when he returned my salutation with that cavalier air which stamps your six-year-old man of the world, there was an intonation in his voice so curiously like Prue's, that I laughed all to myself!

A RIVERMOUTH ROMANCE

A RIVERMOUTH ROMANCE

I

At five o'clock on the morning of the 10th of July, 1860, the front door of a certain house on Anchor Street, in the ancient seaport town of Rivermouth, might have been observed to open with great caution. This door, as the least imaginative reader may easily conjecture, did not open itself. It was opened by Miss Margaret Callaghan, who immediately closed it softly behind her, paused for a few seconds with an embarrassed air on the stone step, and then, throwing a furtive glance up at the second-story windows, passed hastily down the street towards the river, keeping close to the fences and garden walls on her left.

There was a ghost-like stealthiness to Miss Margaret's movements, though there was nothing whatever of the ghost about Miss Margaret herself. She was a plump, short person, no longer young, with coal-black hair growing low on the forehead, and a round face that would have been nearly meaningless if the features had not been emphasized — italicized, so to speak — by the small-pox. Moreover, the brilliancy of her toilet would have rendered any ghostly hypothesis untenable. Mrs. Solomon (we refer to the dressiest Mrs. Solomon, whichever one that was) in all her glory was not arrayed like Miss Margaret on that eventful summer morning. She wore a light green, shot-silk frock, a blazing red shawl, and a yellow crape bonnet profusely decorated with azure, orange, and magenta artificial flowers. In her hand she carried a white parasol. The newly risen sun, ricochetting from the bosom of the river and striking point-blank on the topknot of Miss Margaret's gorgeousness, made her an imposing spectacle in the quiet street of that Puritan village. But, in spite of the bravery of her apparel, she stole guiltily along by garden walls and fences until she reached a small, dingy frame house near the wharves, in the darkened doorway of which she quenched her burning splendor, if so bold a figure is permissible.

Three quarters of an hour passed. The sunshine moved slowly up Anchor Street, fingered noiselessly the well-kept brass knockers on either side, and drained the heel-taps of dew which had been left from the revels of the fairies overnight in the cups of the morning-glories. Not a soul was stirring yet in this part of the town, though the Rivermouthians are such early birds that not a worm may be said to escape them. By and by one of the brown Holland shades at one of the upper windows of the Bilkins mansion — the house from which Miss Margaret had emerged — was drawn up, and old Mr. Bilkins in spiral nightcap looked out on the sunny street. Not a living creature was to be seen, save the dissipated family cat — a very Lovelace of a cat that was not allowed a night-key — who was patiently sitting on the curbstone opposite, waiting for the hall door to be opened. Three quarters of an hour, we repeat, had passed, when Mrs. Margaret O'Rourke, *née* Callaghan, issued from the small, dingy house by the river, and regained the doorstep of the Bilkins mansion in the same stealthy fashion in which she had left it.

Not to prolong a mystery that must already oppress the reader, Mr. Bilkins's cook had, after the manner of her kind, stolen out of the premises before the family were up, and got herself married — surreptitiously and artfully married, as if matrimony were an indictable offence.

And something of an offence it was in this instance. In the first place Margaret Callaghan had lived nearly twenty years with the Bilkins family, and the old folks — there were no children now — had rewarded this long service by taking Margaret into their affections. It was a piece of subtile ingratitude for her to marry without admitting the worthy couple to her confidence. In the next place, Margaret had married a man some eighteen years younger than herself. That was the young man's lookout, you say. We hold it was Margaret that was to blame. What does a young blade of twenty-two know? Not half so much as he thinks he does. His exhaustless ignorance at that age is a discovery which is left for him to make in his prime.

> "Curly gold locks cover foolish brains,
>   Billing and cooing is all your cheer;
> Sighing and singing of midnight strains,
>   Under Bonnybell's window-panes —
>   Wait till you come to Forty Year!"

In one sense Margaret's husband *had* come to forty year — she was forty to a day.

Mrs. Margaret O'Rourke, with the baddish cat following closely at her heels, entered the Bilkins mansion, reached her chamber in the attic without being intercepted, and there laid aside her finery. Two or three times, while arranging her more humble attire, she paused to take a look at the marriage certificate, which she had deposited between the leaves of her prayer book, and on each occasion held that potent document upside down; for Margaret's literary culture was of the severest order, and excluded the art of reading.

The breakfast was late that morning. As Mrs. O'Rourke set the coffee-urn in front of Mrs. Bilkins and flanked Mr. Bilkins with the broiled mackerel and buttered toast, Mrs. O'Rourke's conscience smote her. She afterwards declared that when she saw the two sitting there so innocent-like, not dreaming of the *comether* she had put upon them, she secretly and unbeknownt let a few tears fall into the cream-pitcher. Whether or not it was this material expression of Margaret's penitence that spoiled the coffee does not admit of inquiry; but the coffee was bad. In fact, the whole breakfast was a comedy of errors.

It was a blessed relief to Margaret when the meal was ended. She retired in a cold perspiration to the penetralia of the kitchen, and it was remarked by both Mr. and Mrs. Bilkins that those short flights of vocalism — apropos of the personal charms of one Kate Kearney who lived on the banks of Killarney — which ordinarily issued from the direction of the scullery were unheard that forenoon.

The town clock was striking eleven, and the

antiquated timepiece on the staircase (which never spoke but it dropped pearls and crystals, like the fairy in the story) was lisping the hour, when there came three tremendous knocks at the street-door. Mrs. Bilkins, who was dusting the brass-mounted chronometer in the hall, stood transfixed, with arm uplifted. The admirable old lady had for years been carrying on a guerrilla warfare with itinerant venders of furniture polish, and pain-killer, and crockery cement, and the like. The effrontery of the triple knock convinced her the enemy was at her gates — possibly that dissolute creature with twenty-four sheets of note-paper and twenty-four envelopes for fifteen cents.

Mrs. Bilkins swept across the hall, and opened the door with a jerk. The suddenness of the movement was apparently not anticipated by the person outside, who, with one arm stretched feebly towards the receding knocker, tilted gently forward, and rested both hands on the threshold in an attitude which was probably common enough with our ancestors of the Simian period, but could never have been considered graceful. By an effort that testified to the excellent condition of his muscles, the person instantly righted himself, and stood swaying unsteadily on his toes and heels, and smiling rather vaguely on Mrs. Bilkins.

It was a slightly built but well-knitted young fellow, in the not unpicturesque garb of our marine service. His woollen cap, pitched forward at an acute angle with his nose, showed the back part of a head thatched with short yellow hair, which had broken into innumerable curls of painful tightness. On his ruddy cheeks a sparse sandy beard was making a timid début. Add to this a weak, good-natured mouth, a pair of devil-may-care blue eyes, and the fact that the man was very drunk, and you have a pre-Raphaelite portrait — we may as well say it at once — of Mr. Larry O'Rourke of Mullingar, County Westmeath, and late of the United States sloop of war Santee.

The man was a total stranger to Mrs. Bilkins; but the instant she caught sight of the double white anchors embroidered on the lapels of his jacket, she unhesitatingly threw back the door, which with great presence of mind she had partly closed.

A drunken sailor standing on the step of the Bilkins mansion was no novelty. The street, as we have stated, led down to the wharves, and sailors were constantly passing. The house abutted directly on the street; the granite doorstep was almost flush with the sidewalk, and the huge old-fashioned brass knocker — seemingly a brazen hand that had been cut off at the wrist, and nailed against the oak as a warning to malefactors — extended itself in a kind of grim appeal to everybody. It seemed to possess strange fascinations for all seafaring folk; and when there was a man-of-war in port the rat-tat-tat of that knocker would frequently startle the quiet neighborhood long after midnight. There appeared to be an occult understanding between it and the blue-jackets. Years ago there was a young Bilkins, one Pendexter Bilkins — a sad losel, we fear — who ran away to try his fortunes before the mast, and fell overboard in a gale off Hatteras. "Lost at sea," says the chubby marble slab in the Old South Burying-Ground, "*ætat* 18." Perhaps that is why no blue-jacket, sober or drunk, was ever repulsed from the door of the Bilkins mansion.

Of course Mrs. Bilkins had her taste in the matter, and preferred them sober. But as this could not always be, she tempered her wind, so to speak, to the shorn lamb. The flushed, prematurely old face that now looked up at her moved the good lady's pity.

"What do you want?" she asked kindly.

"Me wife."

"There's no wife for you here," said Mrs. Bilkins, somewhat taken aback. "His wife!" she thought; "it's a mother the poor boy stands in need of."

A RIVERMOUTH ROMANCE

"Me wife," repeated Mr. O'Rourke, "for betther or for worse."

"You had better go away," said Mrs. Bilkins, bridling, "or it will be the worse for you."

"To have and to howld," continued Mr. O'Rourke, wandering retrospectively in the mazes of the marriage service, "to have and to howld, till death — bad luck to him! — takes one or the ither of us."

"You're a blasphemous creature," said Mrs. Bilkins severely.

"Thim's the words his riverince spake this mornin', standin' foreninst us," explained Mr. O'Rourke. "I stood here, see, and me jew'l stood there, and the howly chaplain beyont."

And Mr. O'Rourke with a wavering forefinger drew a diagram of the interesting situation on the doorstep.

"Well," returned Mrs. Bilkins, "if you're a married man, all I have to say is, there's a pair of fools instead of one. You had better be off; the person you want does n't live here."

"Bedad, thin, but she does."

"Lives here?"

"Sorra a place else."

"The man's crazy," said Mrs. Bilkins to herself.

While she thought him simply drunk she

was not in the least afraid ; but the idea that she was conversing with a madman sent a chill over her. She reached back her hand preparatory to shutting the door, when Mr. O'Rourke, with an agility that might have been expected from his previous gymnastics, set one foot on the threshold and frustrated the design.

"I want me wife," he said sternly.

Unfortunately, Mr. Bilkins had gone up town, and there was no one in the house except Margaret, whose pluck was not to be depended on. The case was urgent. With the energy of despair Mrs. Bilkins suddenly placed the toe of her boot against Mr. O'Rourke's invading foot, and pushed it away. The effect of this attack was to cause Mr. O'Rourke to describe a semicircle on one leg, and then sit down heavily on the threshold. The lady retreated to the hat-stand, and rested her hand mechanically on the handle of a blue cotton umbrella. Mr. O'Rourke partly turned his head and smiled upon her with conscious superiority. At this juncture a third actor appeared on the scene, evidently a friend of Mr. O'Rourke's, for he addressed that gentleman as "a spalpeen," and told him to go home.

"Divil an inch," replied the spalpeen ; but he got himself off the threshold, and resumed his position on the step.

"It's only Larry, mum," said the man, touching his forelock politely; "as dacent a lad as iver lived, when he's not in liquor; an' I've known him to be sober for days togither," he added reflectively. "He don't mane a ha'p'orth o' harum, but jist now he's not quite in his right moind."

"I should think not," said Mrs. Bilkins, turning from the speaker to Mr. O'Rourke, who had seated himself gravely on the scraper, and was weeping. "Hasn't the man any friends?"

"Too many of 'em, mum, an' it's along wid dhrinkin' toasts wid 'em that Larry got throwed. The punch that spalpeen has dhrunk this day would amaze ye. He give us the slip awhiles ago, bad 'cess to him, an' come up here. Didn't I tell ye, Larry, not to be afther ringin' at the owld gintleman's knocker? Ain't ye got no sinse at all?"

"Misther Donnehugh," responded Mr. O'Rourke, with great dignity, "ye're dhrunk agin."

Mr. Donnehugh, who had not taken more than thirteen ladles of rum-punch, disdained to reply directly.

"He's a dacent lad enough" — this to Mrs. Bilkins — "but his head is wake. Whin he's had two sups o' whiskey he belaves he's dhrunk a bar'l full. A gill o' wather out of a jimmy-john'd fuddle him, mum."

"Is n't there anybody to look after him?"

"No, mum, he's an orphan; his father and mother live in the owld counthry, an' a fine hale owld couple they are."

"Has n't he any family in the town" —

"Sure, mum, he has a family; was n't he married this blessed mornin'?"

"He said so."

"Indade, thin, he was — the pore divil!"

"And the — the person?" inquired Mrs. Bilkins.

"Is it the wife, ye mane?"

"Yes, the wife: where is she?"

"Well, thin, mum," said Mr. Donnehugh, "it's yerself can answer that."

"I?" exclaimed Mrs. Bilkins. "Good heavens! this man's as crazy as the other!"

"Begorra, if anybody's crazy, it's Larry, for it's Larry has married Margaret."

"What Margaret?" cried Mrs. Bilkins, with a start.

"Margaret Callaghan, sure."

"*Our* Margaret? Do you mean to say that OUR Margaret has married that — that good-for-nothing, inebriated wretch!"

"It's a civil tongue the owld lady has, anyway," remarked Mr. O'Rourke critically, from the scraper.

Mrs. Bilkins's voice during the latter part of

the colloquy had been pitched in a high key; it rung through the hall and penetrated to the kitchen, where Margaret was thoughtfully wiping the breakfast things. She paused with a half-dried saucer in her hand, and listened. In a moment more she stood, with bloodless face and limp figure, leaning against the banister, behind Mrs. Bilkins.

"Is it there ye are, me jew'l!" cried Mr. O'Rourke, discovering her.

Mrs. Bilkins wheeled upon Margaret.

"Margaret Callaghan, *is* that thing your husband?"

"Ye-yes, mum," faltered Mrs. O'Rourke, with a woful lack of spirit.

"Then take it away!" cried Mrs. Bilkins.

Margaret, with a slight flush on either cheek, glided past Mrs. Bilkins, and the heavy oak door closed with a bang, as the gates of Paradise must have closed of old upon Adam and Eve.

"Come!" said Margaret, taking Mr. O'Rourke by the hand; and the two wandered forth upon their wedding journey down Anchor Street, with all the world before them where to choose. They chose to halt at the small, shabby tenement-house by the river, through the doorway of which the bridal pair disappeared with a reeling, eccentric gait; for Mr.

O'Rourke's intoxication seemed to have run down his elbow, and communicated itself to Margaret.

O Hymen! who burnest precious gums and scented woods in thy torch at the melting of aristocratic hearts, with what a pitiful penny-dip thou hast lighted up our little back-street romance!

II

It had been no part of Margaret's plan to acknowledge the marriage so soon. Though on pleasure bent, she had a frugal mind. She had invested in a husband with a view of laying him away for a rainy day — that is to say, for such a time as her master and mistress should cease to need her services; for she had promised on more than one occasion to remain with the old couple as long as they lived. Indeed, if Mr. O'Rourke had come to her and said in so many words, "The day you marry me you must leave the Bilkins family," there is very little doubt but Margaret would have let that young sea-monster slip back unmated, so far as she was concerned, into his native element. The contingency never entered into her calculations. She intended that the ship which had brought Ulysses to her island should take him off again after a decent interval of honeymoon; then she would confess all to Mrs. Bilkins, and be forgiven, and Mr. Bilkins would not cancel that clause supposed to exist in his will bequeathing two first-mortgage bonds of the Eastern Railroad to a certain faithful servant. In the meanwhile she would add each month to the store in the coffers of the Rivermouth Savings Bank; for Calypso had a neat sum to her credit on the books of that provident institution.

But this could not be now. The volatile bridegroom had upset the wisely conceived plan, and "all the fat was in the fire," as Margaret philosophically put it. Mr. O'Rourke had been fully instructed in the part he was to play, and, to do him justice, had honestly intended to play it; but destiny was against him. It may be observed that destiny and Mr. O'Rourke were not on very friendly terms.

After the ceremony had been performed and Margaret had stolen back to the Bilkins mansion, as related, Mr. O'Rourke with his own skilful hands had brewed a noble punch for the wedding guests. Standing at the head of the table and stirring the pungent mixture in a small wash-tub purchased for the occasion, Mr. O'Rourke came out in full flower. His flow of wit, as he replenished the glasses, was as racy and seemingly as inexhaustible as the punch itself. When Mrs. McLaughlin held out her glass, inadvertently upside down, for her sixth ladleful, Mr. O'Rourke gallantly declared it should be filled if he had to stand on his head to do it. The elder Miss O'Leary whispered to Mrs. Connolly that Mr. O'Rourke was "a perfic gintleman," and the men in a body pronounced him a bit of the raal shamrock. If Mr. O'Rourke was happy in brewing a punch, he was happier in dispensing it, and happiest of all in drinking a great deal of it himself. He toasted Mrs. Finnigan, the landlady, and the late lamented Finnigan, the father, whom he had never seen, and Miss Biddy Finnigan, the daughter, and a young toddling Finnigan, who was at large in shockingly scant raiment. He drank to the company individually and collectively, drank to the absent, drank to a tin-pedler who chanced to pass the window, and indeed was in that propitiatory mood when he would have drunk to the health of each separate animal that came out of the Ark. It was in the midst of the confusion and applause which followed his song, The Wearin' of the Grane, that Mr. O'Rourke, the punch being all gone, withdrew unobserved, and went in quest of Mrs. O'Rourke — with what success the reader knows.

According to the love-idyl of the period, when Laura and Charles Henry, after unheard-of obstacles, are finally united, all cares and tribulations and responsibilities slip from their sleek backs like Christian's burden. The idea is a pretty one, theoretically, but, like some of those models in the Patent Office at Washington, it fails to work. Charles Henry does not go on sitting at Laura's feet and reading Tennyson to her forever: the rent of the cottage by the sea falls due with prosaic regularity; there are bakers, and butchers, and babies, and tax-collectors, and doctors, and undertakers, and sometimes gentlemen of the jury, to be attended to. Wedded life is not one long amatory poem with recurrent rhymes of love and dove, and kiss and bliss. Yet when the average sentimental novelist has supplied his hero and heroine with their bridal outfit and arranged that little matter of the marriage certificate, he usually turns off the gas, puts up his shutters, and saunters off with his hands in his pockets, as if the day's business were over. But we, who are honest dealers in real life and disdain to give short weight, know better. The business is by no means over; it is just begun. It is not Christian throwing off his pack for good and all, but Christian taking up a load heavier and more difficult than any he has carried.

If Margaret Callaghan, when she meditated matrimony, indulged in any roseate dreams, they were quickly put to flight. She suddenly found herself dispossessed of a quiet, comfortable home, and face to face with the fact that she had a white elephant on her hands. It is not likely that Mr. O'Rourke assumed precisely the shape of a white elephant to her mental vision; but he was as useless and cumbersome and unmanageable as one.

Margaret and Larry's wedding tour did not extend beyond Mrs. Finnigan's establishment, where they took two or three rooms and set up housekeeping in a humble way. Margaret, who was a tidy housewife, kept the floor of her apartments as white as your hand, the tin plates on the dresser as bright as your ladylove's eyes, and the cooking-stove as neat as the machinery on a Sound steamer. When she was not rubbing the stove with lampblack she was cooking upon it some savory dish to tempt the palate of her marine monster. Naturally of a hopeful temperament, she went about her work singing softly to herself at times, and would have been very happy that first week if Mr. O'Rourke had known a sober moment. But Mr. O'Rourke showed an exasperating disposition to keep up festivities. At the end of ten days, however, he toned down, and at Margaret's suggestion that he had better be looking about for some employment he rigged up a fishing-pole, and set out with an injured air for the wharf at the foot of the street, where he fished for the rest of the day. To sit for hours blinking in the sun, waiting for a cunner to come along and take his hook, was as exhaustive a kind of labor as he cared to engage in. Though Mr. O'Rourke had recently returned from a long cruise, he had not a cent to show. During his first three days ashore he had dissipated his three years' pay. The housekeeping expenses began eating a hole in Margaret's little fund, the existence of which was no sooner known to Mr. O'Rourke than he stood up his fishing-rod in one corner of the room, and thenceforth it caught nothing but cobwebs.

"Divil a sthroke o' work I'll do," said Mr. O'Rourke, "whin we can live at aise on our earnin's. Who'd be afther frettin' hisself, wid money in the bank? How much is it, Peggy darlint?"

And divil a stroke more of work did he do. He lounged down on the wharves, and, with his short clay pipe stuck between his lips and his hands in his pockets, stared off at the sailboats on the river. He sat on the doorstep of the Finnigan domicile, and plentifully chaffed the passers-by. Now and then, when he could wheedle some fractional currency out of Margaret, he spent it like a crown prince at The

Wee Drop around the corner. With that fine magnetism which draws together birds of a feather, he shortly drew about him all the ne'er-do-weels of Rivermouth. It was really wonderful what an unsuspected lot of them there was. From all the frowzy purlieus of the town they crept forth into the sunlight to array themselves under the banner of the prince of scallawags. It was edifying of a summer afternoon to see a dozen of them sitting in a row, like turtles, on the string-piece of Jedediah Rand's wharf, with their twenty-four feet dangling over the water, assisting Mr. O'Rourke in contemplating the islands in the harbor, and upholding the scenery, as it were.

The rascal had one accomplishment, he had a heavenly voice — quite in the rough, to be sure — and he played on the violin like an angel. He did not know one note from another, but he played in a sweet natural way, just as Orpheus must have played, by ear. The drunker he was the more pathos and humor he wrung from the old violin, his sole piece of personal property. He had a singular fancy for getting up at two or three o'clock in the morning, and playing by an open casement, to the distraction of all the dogs in the immediate neighborhood and innumerable dogs in the distance.

Unfortunately, Mr. O'Rourke's freaks were

not always of so innocent a complexion. On one or two occasions, through an excess of animal and other spirits, he took to breaking windows in the town. Among his nocturnal feats he accomplished the demolition of the glass in the door of The Wee Drop. Now, breaking windows in Rivermouth is an amusement not wholly disconnected with an interior view of the police-station (bridewell is the local term); so it happened that Mr. O'Rourke woke up one fine morning and found himself snug and tight in one of the cells in the rear of the Brick Market. His plea that the bull's-eye in the glass door of The Wee Drop winked at him in an insultin' manner as he was passing by did not prevent Justice Hackett from fining the delinquent ten dollars and costs, which made sad havoc with the poor wife's bank account. So Margaret's married life wore on, and all went merry as a funeral knell.

After Mrs. Bilkins, with a brow as severe as that of one of the Parcæ, had closed the door upon the O'Rourkes that summer morning, she sat down on the stairs, and, sinking the indignant goddess in the woman, burst into tears. She was still very wroth with Margaret Callaghan, as she persisted in calling her; very merciless and unforgiving, as the gentler sex are apt to be — to the gentler sex. Mr. Bilkins, however, after the first vexation, missed Margaret from the household; missed her singing, which was in itself as helpful as a second girl; missed her hand in the preparation of those hundred and one nameless comforts which are necessities to the old, and wished in his soul that he had her back again. Who could make a gruel, when he was ill, or cook a steak, when he was well, like Margaret? So, meeting her one morning at the fish-market — for Mr. O'Rourke had long since given over the onerous labor of catching cunners — he spoke to her kindly, and asked her how she liked the change in her life, and if Mr. O'Rourke was good to her.

"Troth, thin, sur," said Margaret, with a short, dry laugh, "he's the divil's own!"

Margaret was thin and careworn, and her laugh had the mild gayety of champagne not properly corked. These things were apparent even to Mr. Bilkins, who was not a shrewd observer.

"I'm afraid, Margaret," he remarked sorrowfully, "that you are not making both ends meet."

"Begorra, I'd be glad if I could make one ind meet!" returned Margaret.

With a duplicity quite foreign to his nature, Mr. Bilkins gradually drew from her the true state of affairs. Mr. O'Rourke was a very bad case indeed; he did nothing towards her support; he was almost constantly drunk; the little money she had laid by was melting away, and would not last until winter. Mr. O'Rourke was perpetually coming home with a sprained ankle, or a bruised shoulder, or a broken head. He had broken most of the furniture in his festive hours, including the cooking-stove. "In short," as Mr. Bilkins said in relating the matter afterwards to Mrs. Bilkins, "he had broken all those things which he shouldn't have broken, and failed to break the one thing he ought to have broken long ago — his neck, namely."

The revelation which startled Mr. Bilkins most was this: in spite of all, Margaret loved Larry with the whole of her warm Irish heart. Further than keeping the poor creature up waiting for him until ever so much o'clock at night, it did not appear that he treated her with personal cruelty. If he had beaten her, perhaps she would have worshipped him. It needed only that.

Revolving Margaret's troubles in his thoughts as he walked homeward, Mr. Bilkins struck upon a plan by which he could help her. When this plan was laid before Mrs. Bilkins, she opposed it with a vehemence that convinced him she had made up her mind to adopt it.

"Never, never will I have that ungrateful woman under this roof!" cried Mrs. Bilkins; and accordingly the next day Mr. and Mrs. O'Rourke took up their abode in the Bilkins mansion — Margaret as cook, and Larry as gardener.

"I'm convenient, if the owld gintleman is," had been Mr. O'Rourke's remark, when the proposition was submitted to him. Not that Mr. O'Rourke had the faintest idea of gardening. He didn't know a tulip from a tomato. He was one of those sanguine persons who never hesitate to undertake anything, and are never abashed by their herculean inability.

Mr. Bilkins did not look to Margaret's husband for any great botanical knowledge; but he was rather surprised one day when Mr. O'Rourke pointed to the triangular bed of lilies-of-the-valley, then out of flower, and remarked, "Thim's a nate lot o' purtaties ye've got there, sur." Mr. Bilkins, we repeat, did not expect much from Mr. O'Rourke's skill in gardening; his purpose was to reform the fellow if possible, and in any case to make Margaret's lot easier.

Reëstablished in her old home, Margaret broke into song again, and Mr. O'Rourke himself promised to do very well; morally, we mean, not agriculturally. His ignorance of the simplest laws of nature, if nature has any simple laws, and his dense stupidity on every other subject were heavy trials to Mr. Bilkins. Happily, Mr. Bilkins was not without a sense of humor, else he would have found Mr. O'Rourke insupportable. Just when the old gentleman's patience was about exhausted, the gardener would commit some atrocity so perfectly comical that his master all but loved him for the moment.

"Larry," said Mr. Bilkins, one breathless afternoon in the middle of September, "just see how the thermometer on the back porch stands."

Mr. O'Rourke disappeared, and after a prolonged absence returned with the monstrous announcement that the thermometer stood at 820!

Mr. Bilkins looked at the man closely. He was unmistakably sober.

"Eight hundred and twenty what?" cried Mr. Bilkins, feeling very warm, as he naturally would in so high a temperature.

"Eight hundthred an' twinty degrays, I suppose, sur."

"Larry, you're an idiot."

This was obviously not to Mr. O'Rourke's taste; for he went out and brought the thermometer, and, pointing triumphantly to the

A RIVERMOUTH ROMANCE

line of numerals running parallel with the glass tube, exclaimed, "Add 'em up yerself, thin!"

Perhaps this would not have been amusing if Mr. Bilkins had not spent the greater part of the previous forenoon in initiating Mr. O'Rourke into the mysteries of the thermometer. Nothing could make amusing Mr. O'Rourke's method of setting out crocus bulbs. Mr. Bilkins had received a lot of a very choice variety from Boston, and having a headache that morning, turned over to Mr. O'Rourke the duty of planting them. Though he had never seen a bulb in his life, Larry unblushingly asserted that he had set out thousands for Sir Lucius O'Grady of O'Grady Castle, "an illegant place intirely, wid tin miles o' garden-walks," added Mr. O'Rourke, crushing Mr. Bilkins, who boasted only of a few humble flower-beds.

The following day he stepped into the garden to see how Larry had done his work. There stood the parched bulbs, carefully arranged in circles and squares on top of the soil.

"Did n't I tell you to set out these bulbs?" cried Mr. Bilkins wrathfully.

"An' did n't I set 'em out?" expostulated Mr. O'Rourke. "An' ain't they a settin' there beautiful?"

"But you should have put them into the ground, stupid!"

"Is it bury 'em ye mane? Be jabbers! how could they iver git out agin? Give the little jokers a fair show, Misther Bilkins!"

For two weeks Mr. O'Rourke conducted himself with comparative propriety; that is to say, he rendered himself useless about the place, appeared regularly at his meals, and kept sober. Perhaps the hilarious strains of music which sometimes issued at midnight from the upper window of the north gable were not just what a quiet, unostentatious family would desire; but on the whole there was not much to complain of.

The third week witnessed a falling off. Though always promptly on hand at the serving out of rations, Mr. O'Rourke did not even make a pretence of working in the garden. He would disappear mysteriously immediately after breakfast, and reappear with supernatural abruptness at dinner. Nobody knew what he did with himself in the interval, until one day he was observed to fall out of an apple-tree near the stable. His retreat discovered, he took to the wharves and the alleys in the distant part of the town. It soon became evident that his ways were not the ways of temperance, and that all his paths led to The Wee Drop.

A RIVERMOUTH ROMANCE

Of course Margaret tried to keep this from the family. Being a woman, she coined excuses for him in her heart. It was a dull life for the lad, anyway, and it was worse than him that was leading Larry astray. Hours and hours after the old couple had gone to bed, she would sit without a light in the lonely kitchen, listening for that shuffling step along the gravel walk. Night after night she never closed her eyes, and went about the house the next day with that smooth, impenetrable face behind which women hide their care.

One morning found Margaret sitting pale and anxious by the kitchen stove. O'Rourke had not come home at all. Noon came, and night, but not Larry. Whenever Mrs. Bilkins approached her that day, Margaret was humming Kate Kearney quite merrily. But when her work was done, she stole out at the back gate and went in search of him. She scoured the neighborhood like a mad-woman. O'Rourke had not been at the Finnigans'. He had not been at The Wee Drop since Monday, and this was Wednesday night. Her heart sunk within her when she failed to find him in the police-station. Some dreadful thing had happened to him. She came back to the house with one hand pressed wearily against her cheek. The dawn struggled through the kitchen windows, and fell upon Margaret crouched by the stove.

She could no longer wear her mask. When Mr. Bilkins came down she confessed that Larry had taken to drinking again, and had not been home for two nights.

"Mayhap he's drownded hisself," suggested Margaret, wringing her hands.

"Not he," said Mr. Bilkins; "he does n't like the taste of water well enough."

"Troth, thin, he does n't," reflected Margaret, and the reflection comforted her.

"At any rate, I'll go and look him up after breakfast," said Mr. Bilkins. And after breakfast, accordingly, Mr. Bilkins sallied forth with the depressing expectation of finding Mr. O'Rourke without much difficulty. "Come to think of it," said the old gentleman to himself, drawing on his white cotton gloves as he walked up Anchor Street, "*I* don't want to find him."

III

But Mr. O'Rourke was not to be found. With amiable cynicism Mr. Bilkins directed his steps in the first instance to the police-station, quite confident that a bird of Mr. O'Rourke's plumage would be brought to perch in such a cage. But not so much as a feather of him was discoverable. The Wee Drop was not the only bacchanalian resort in Rivermouth; there were five or six other low drinking-shops scattered about town, and through these Mr. Bilkins went conscientiously. He then explored various blind alleys, known haunts of the missing man, and took a careful survey of the wharves along the river on his way home. He even shook the apple-tree near the stable with a vague hope of bringing down Mr. O'Rourke, but brought down nothing except a few winter apples, which, being both unripe and unsound, were not perhaps bad representatives of the object of his search.

That evening a small boy stopped at the door of the Bilkins mansion with a straw hat, at once identified as Mr. O'Rourke's, which had been found on Neal's Wharf. This would have told against another man; but O'Rourke was always leaving his hat on a wharf. Margaret's distress is not to be pictured. She fell back upon and clung to the idea that Larry had drowned himself, not intentionally, may be; possibly he had fallen overboard while intoxicated.

The late Mr. Buckle has informed us that death by drowning is regulated by laws as inviolable and beautiful as those of the solar system; that a certain percentage of the earth's population is bound to drown itself annually, whether it wants to or not. It may be presumed, then, that Rivermouth's proper quota of dead bodies was washed ashore during the ensuing two months. There had been gales off the coast and pleasure parties on the river, and between them they had managed to do a ghastly business. But Mr. O'Rourke failed to appear among the flotsam and jetsam which the receding tides left tangled in the piles of the Rivermouth wharves. This convinced Margaret that Larry had proved a too tempting morsel to some buccaneering shark, or had fallen a victim to one of those immense schools of fish which seem to have a yearly appointment with the fishermen on this coast. From that day Margaret never saw a cod or a

A RIVERMOUTH ROMANCE

mackerel brought into the house without an involuntary shudder. She averted her head in making up the fish-balls, as if she half dreaded to detect a faint aroma of whiskey about them. And, indeed, why might not a man fall into the sea, be eaten, say, by a halibut, and reappear on the scene of his earthly triumphs and defeats in the non-committal form of hashed fish?

> "Imperial Cæsar, dead and turned to clay,
> Might stop a hole to keep the wind away."

But, perhaps, as the conservative Horatio suggests, 't were to consider too curiously to consider so.

Mr. Bilkins had come to adopt Margaret's explanation of O'Rourke's disappearance. He was undoubtedly drowned; had most likely drowned himself. The hat picked up on the wharf was strong circumstantial evidence in that direction. But one feature of the case staggered Mr. Bilkins. O'Rourke's violin had also disappeared. Now, it required no great effort to imagine a man throwing himself overboard under the influence of *mania à potu;* but it was difficult to conceive of a man committing violinicide! If the fellow went to drown himself, why did he take his fiddle with him? He might as well have taken an umbrella or a German student-lamp. This question troubled Mr. Bilkins a good deal first and last. But one thing was indisputable: the man was gone — and had evidently gone by water.

It was now that Margaret invested her husband with charms of mind and person not calculated to make him recognizable by any one who had ever had the privilege of knowing him in the faulty flesh. She eliminated all his bad qualities, and projected from her imagination a Mr. O'Rourke as he ought to have been — a species of seraphic being mixed up in some way with a violin; and to this ideal she erected a neat head-stone in the suburban cemetery. "It would be a proud day for Larry," observed Margaret contemplatively, "if he could rest his oi on the illegant monumint I 've put up to him." If Mr. O'Rourke could have read the inscription on it, he would never have suspected his own complicity in the matter.

But there the marble stood, sacred to his memory; and soon the snow came down from the gray sky and covered it, and the invisible snow of weeks and months drifted down on Margaret's heart, and filled up its fissures, and smoothed off the sharp angles of its grief; and there was peace upon it.

Not but she sorrowed for Larry at times.

Yet life had a relish to it again ; she was free, though she did not look at it in that light; she was happier in a quiet fashion than she had ever been, though she would not have acknowledged it to herself. She wondered that she had the heart to laugh when the iceman made love to her. Perhaps she was conscious of something comically incongruous in the warmth of a gentleman who spent all winter in cutting ice, and all summer in dealing it out to his customers. She had not the same excuse for laughing at the baker ; yet she laughed still more merrily at him when he pressed her hand over the steaming loaf of brown-bread, delivered every Saturday morning at the scullery door. Both these gentlemen had known Margaret many years, yet neither of them had valued her very highly until another man came along and married her. A widow, it would appear, is esteemed in some sort as a warranted article, being stamped with the maker's name.

There was even a third lover in prospect ; for according to the gossip of the town, Mr. Donnehugh was frequently to be seen of a Sunday afternoon standing in the cemetery and regarding Mr. O'Rourke's head-stone with unrestrained satisfaction.

A year had passed away, and certain bits

of color blossoming among Margaret's weeds indicated that the winter of her mourning was over. The iceman and the baker were hating each other cordially, and Mrs. Bilkins was daily expecting it would be discovered before night that Margaret had married one or both of them. But to do Margaret justice, she was faithful in thought and deed to the memory of O'Rourke — not the O'Rourke who disappeared so strangely, but the O'Rourke who never existed.

"D' ye think, mum," she said one day to Mrs. Bilkins, as that lady was adroitly sounding her on the ice question — "d' ye think I'd condescind to take up wid the likes o' him, or the baker either, afther sich a man as Larry?"

The rectified and clarified O'Rourke was a permanent wonder to Mr. Bilkins, who bore up under the bereavement with noticeable resignation.

"Peggy is right," said the old gentleman, who was superintending the burning out of the kitchen flue. "She won't find another man like Larry O'Rourke in a hurry."

"Thrue for ye, Mr. Bilkins," answered Margaret. "May be there's as good fish in the say as iver was caught, but I don't belave it, all the same."

As good fish in the sea! The words recalled to Margaret the nature of her loss, and she went on with her work in silence.

"What — what is it, Ezra?" cried Mrs. Bilkins, changing color, and rising hastily from the breakfast-table. Her first thought was of apoplexy.

There sat Mr. Bilkins, with his wig pushed back from his forehead, and his eyes fixed vacantly on The Weekly Chronicle, which he held out at arm's length before him.

"Good heavens, Ezra! what *is* the matter?"

Mr. Bilkins turned his glassy eyes upon her mechanically, as if he were a great wax doll, and somebody had pulled his wire.

"Can't you speak, Ezra?"

His lips opened, and moved inarticulately; then he pointed a rigid finger, in the manner of a guide-board, at a paragraph in the paper, which he held up for Mrs. Bilkins to read over his shoulder. When she had read it she sunk back into her chair without a word, and the two sat contemplating each other as if they had never met before in this world, and were not overpleased at meeting.

The paragraph which produced this singular effect on the aged couple occurred at the end of a column of telegraph despatches giving the details of an unimportant engagement that had just taken place between one of the blockading squadron and a Confederate cruiser. The engagement itself does not concern us, but this item from the list of casualties on the Union side has a direct bearing on our narrative —

"Larry O'Rourke, seaman, splinter wound in the leg. Not serious."

That splinter flew far. It glanced from Mr. O'Rourke's leg, went plumb through the Bilkins mansion, and knocked over a small marble slab in the Old South Burying-Ground.

If a ghost had dropped in familiarly to breakfast, the constraint and consternation of the Bilkins family could not have been greater. How was the astounding intelligence to be broken to Margaret? Her explosive Irish nature made the task one of extreme delicacy. Mrs. Bilkins flatly declared herself incapable of undertaking it. Mr. Bilkins, with many misgivings as to his fitness, assumed the duty; for it would never do to have the news sprung suddenly upon Margaret by persons outside.

As Mrs. O'Rourke was clearing away the breakfast things, Mr. Bilkins, who had lingered near the window with the newspaper in his hand, coughed once or twice in an unnatural way to show that he was not embarrassed, and began to think that may be it would be best to tell Margaret after dinner. Mrs. Bilkins fathomed his thought with that intuition which renders women terrible, and sent across the room an eye-telegram to this effect, "Now is your time."

"There's been another battle down South, Margaret," said the old gentleman presently, folding up the paper and putting it in his pocket. "A sea-fight this time."

"Sure, an' they're allus fightin' down there."

"But not always with so little damage. There was only one man wounded on our side."

"Pore man! It's sorry we oughter be for his wife an' childer, if he's got any."

"Not badly wounded, you will understand, Margaret — not at all seriously wounded; only a splinter in the leg."

"Faith, thin, a splinter in the leg is no pleasant thing in itself."

"A mere scratch," said Mr. Bilkins lightly, as if he were constantly in the habit of going about with a splinter in his own leg, and found it rather agreeable. "The odd part of the matter is the man's first name. His first name was Larry."

Margaret nodded, as one should say, There's a many Larrys in the world.

"But the oddest part of it," continued Mr. Bilkins in a carelessly sepulchral voice, "is the man's last name."

Something in the tone of his voice made Margaret look at him, and something in the expression of his face caused the blood to fly from Margaret's cheek.

"The man's last name!" she repeated wonderingly.

"Yes, his last name — O'Rourke."

"D' ye mane it?" shrieked Margaret — "d' ye mane it? Glory to God! Oh, worra! worra!"

"Well, Ezra," said Mrs. Bilkins, in one of those spasms of base ingratitude to which even the most perfect women are liable, "you've made nice work of it. You might as well have knocked her down with an axe!"

"But, my dear" —

"Oh, bother! — my smelling-bottle, quick! — second bureau drawer — left-hand side."

Joy never kills; it is a celestial kind of hydrogen of which it seems impossible to get too much at one inhalation. In an hour Margaret was able to converse with comparative calmness on the resuscitation of Larry O'Rourke, whom the firing of a cannon had brought to the

A RIVERMOUTH ROMANCE

surface as if he had been in reality a drowned body.

Now that the whole town was aware of Mr. O'Rourke's fate, his friend Mr. Donnehugh came forward with a statement that would have been of some interest at an earlier period, but was of no service as matters stood, except so far as it assisted in removing from Mr. Bilkins's mind a passing doubt as to whether the Larry O'Rourke of the telegraphic reports was Margaret's scapegrace of a husband. Mr. Donnehugh had known all along that O'Rourke had absconded to Boston by a night train and enlisted in the navy. It was the possession of this knowledge that had made it impossible for Mr. Donnehugh to look at Mr. O'Rourke's gravestone without grinning.

At Margaret's request, and in Margaret's name, Mr. Bilkins wrote three or four letters to O'Rourke, and finally succeeded in extorting an epistle from that gentleman, in which he told Margaret to cheer up, that his fortune was as good as made, and that the day would come when she should ride through the town in her own coach, and no thanks to old flint-head, who pretended to be so fond of her. Mr. Bilkins tried to conjecture who was meant by old flint-head, but was obliged to give it up. Mr. O'Rourke furthermore informed Margaret that he had three hundred dollars prize-money coming to him, and broadly intimated that when he got home he intended to have one of the most extensive blow-outs ever witnessed in Rivermouth.

"Och!" laughed Margaret, "that's jist Larry over agin. The pore lad was allus full of his nonsense an' spirits."

"That he was," said Mr. Bilkins dryly.

Content with the fact that her husband was in the land of the living, Margaret gave herself no trouble over the separation. O'Rourke had shipped for three years; one third of his term of service was past, and two years more, God willing, would see him home again. This was Margaret's view of it. Mr. Bilkins's view of it was not so cheerful. The prospect of Mr. O'Rourke's ultimate return was anything but enchanting. Mr. Bilkins was by no means disposed to kill the fatted calf. He would much rather have killed the Prodigal Son. However, there was always this chance: he might never come back.

The tides rose and fell at the Rivermouth wharves; the summer moonlight and the winter snow, in turn, bleached its quiet streets; and the two years had nearly gone by. In the meantime nothing had been heard of O'Rourke. If he ever received the five or six letters sent to him, he did not fatigue himself by answering them.

"Larry's all right," said hopeful Margaret. "If any harum had come to the gossoon, we'd have knowed it. It's the bad news that we get soonest."

Mr. Bilkins was not so positive about that. It had taken him a whole year to find out that O'Rourke had not drowned himself.

The period of Mr. O'Rourke's enlistment had come to an end. Two months slipped by, and he had neglected to brighten Rivermouth with his presence. There were many things that might have detained him, difficulties in getting his prize-papers or in drawing his pay; but there was no reason why he might not have written. The days were beginning to grow long to Margaret, and vague forebodings of misfortune possessed her.

Perhaps we had better look up Mr. O'Rourke.

He had seen some rough times, during those three years, and some harder work than catching cunners at the foot of Anchor Street, or setting out crocuses in Mr. Bilkins's back garden. He had seen battles and shipwreck, and death in many guises; but they had taught him nothing, as the sequel will show. With his active career in the navy we shall not trouble ourselves; we take him up at a date a little prior to the close of his term of service.

Several months before, he had been transferred from the blockading squadron to a gunboat attached to the fleet operating against the forts defending New Orleans. The forts had fallen, the fleet had passed on to the city, and Mr. O'Rourke's ship lay off in the stream, binding up her wounds. In three days he would receive his discharge, and the papers entitling him to a handsome amount of prize-money in addition to his pay. With noble contempt for so much good fortune, Mr. O'Rourke dropped over the bows of the gunboat one evening and managed to reach the levee. In the city he fell in with some soldiers, and, being of a convivial nature, caroused with them that night, and next day enlisted in a cavalry regiment.

Desertion in the face of the enemy — for, though the city lay under Federal guns, it was still hostile enough — involved the heaviest penalties. O'Rourke was speedily arrested with other deserters, tried by court-martial, and sentenced to death.

The intelligence burst like a shell upon the quiet household in Anchor Street, listening daily for the sound of Larry O'Rourke's footstep on the threshold. It was a heavy load for

A RIVERMOUTH ROMANCE 315

Margaret to bear, after all those years of patient vigil. But the load was to be lightened for her. In consideration of O'Rourke's long service, and in view of the fact that his desertion so near the expiration of his time was an absurdity, the Good President commuted his sentence to imprisonment for life, with loss of prize-money and back pay. Mr. O'Rourke was despatched North, and placed in Moyamensing Prison.

If joy could kill, Margaret would have been a dead woman the day these tidings reached Rivermouth; and Mr. Bilkins himself would have been in a critical condition, for, though he did not want O'Rourke shot or hanged, he was delighted to have him permanently shelved.

After the excitement was over, and this is always the trying time, Margaret accepted the situation philosophically.

"The pore lad's out o' harum's rache, anyway," she reflected. "He can't be gittin' into hot wather now, and that's a fact. And may be after awhiles they'll let him go agin. They let out murtherers and thaves and sich-like, and Larry's done no hurt to nobody but hisself."

Margaret was inclined to be rather severe on President Lincoln for taking away Larry's prize-money. The impression was indelible on her mind that the money went into Mr. Lincoln's private exchequer.

"I wouldn't wonder if Misthress Lincoln had a new silk gownd or two this fall," Margaret would remark sarcastically.

The prison rules permitted Mr. O'Rourke to receive periodical communications from his friends outside. Once every quarter Mr. Bilkins wrote him a letter, and in the interim Margaret kept him supplied with those doleful popular ballads, printed on broadsides, which one sees pinned up for sale on the iron railings of city churchyards, and seldom anywhere else. They seem the natural exhalations of the mould and pathos of such places, but we have a suspicion that they are written by sentimental young undertakers. Though these songs must have been a solace to Mr. O'Rourke in his captivity, he never so far forgot himself as to acknowledge their receipt. It was only through the kindly chaplain of the prison that Margaret was now and then advised of the well-being of her husband.

Towards the close of that year the great O'Rourke himself did condescend to write one letter. As this letter has never been printed, and as it is the only specimen extant of Mr.

O'Rourke's epistolary manner, we lay it before the reader *verbatim et literatim* —

febuary. 1864

mi belovid wife
        fur the luv of God sind mee pop gose the wezel. yours till deth
        larry O rourke.

Pop goes the Weasel was sent to him, and Mr. Bilkins ingeniously slipped into the same envelope The Drunkard's Death and Beware of the Bowl, two spirited compositions well calculated to exert a salutary influence over a man imprisoned for life.

There is nothing in this earthly existence so uncertain as what seems to be a certainty. To all appearances, the world outside of Moyamensing Prison was forever a closed book to O'Rourke. But the Southern Confederacy collapsed, the General Amnesty Proclamation was issued, cell doors were thrown open; and one afternoon Mr. Larry O'Rourke, with his head neatly shaved, walked into the Bilkins kitchen and frightened Margaret nearly out of her skin.

Mr. O'Rourke's summing up of his case was characteristic: "I've been kilt in battle, hanged by the court-martial, put into the lock-up for life, and here I am, bedad, not a ha'p'orth the worse for it."

None the worse for it, certainly, and none the better. By no stretch of magical fiction can we make an angel of him. He is not at all the material for an apotheosis. It was not for him to reform and settle down, and become a respectable, oppressed taxpayer. His conduct in Rivermouth, after his return, was a repetition of his old ways. Margaret all but broke down under the tests to which he put her affections, and came at last to wish that Larry had never got out of Moyamensing Prison.

If any change had taken place in Mr. O'Rourke, it showed itself in occasional fits of sullenness towards Margaret. It was in one of these moods that he slouched his hat over his brows, and told her she need not wait dinner for him. Margaret supposed that this was one of Larry's jokes.

But it will be a cold dinner, if Margaret has kept it waiting; for two years have gone by since that day, and O'Rourke has not come home.

Possibly he is off on a whaling voyage; possibly the swift maelstrom has dragged him down; perhaps he is lifting his hand to knock at the door of the Bilkins mansion as we pen these words. But Margaret does not watch for him impatiently any more. There are strands of gray in her black hair. She has had her romance.

The Riverside Press
CAMBRIDGE . MASSACHUSETTS
U · S · A